FOR GRANDPARENTS
Wonders and Worries

CHRISTIAN CARE BOOKS

Wayne E. Oates, Editor

FOR GRANDPARENTS
Wonders and Worries

by

Myron C. Madden
and
Mary Ben Madden

THE WESTMINSTER PRESS
Philadelphia

Book Design by Dorothy Alden Smith

First edition

Published by The Westminster Press®
Philadelphia, Pennsylvania

PRINTED IN THE UNITED STATES OF AMERICA
9 8 7 6 5 4 3 2 1

Library of Congress Cataloging in Publication Data

Madden, Myron C
   For grandparents.

   (Christian care books ; 9)
   Bibliography: p.
   1. Grandparents—United States. I. Madden,
Mary Ben, joint author. II. Title. III. Series.
HQ759.9.M3   306.8'7   80–12778
ISBN 0–664–24325–8

Contents

Continued

PART II

GRANDPARENTING: A LOOK AT ITS CARES AND CONCERNS

Preface

Mary Ben and I grew up in the same small town and were sweethearts in high school. We have seen our own parents sparkle over our five children. Now we find ourselves losing all objectivity and even rationality about our three grandchildren.

For the purpose of writing this book, we have taken weekends at our place on Bayou Lacombe, some fifty miles from New Orleans. It is there that we most enjoy our grandchildren. They have a chance to ask questions about butterflies, lizards, whippoorwills, fireflies, and spider webs. Yet the bayou is not different from Eden of ancient time; we have serpents, fire ants, mosquitoes, gnats, and fierce bolts of lightning. So the questions we get have to do not only with the good and the beautiful but with the threatening and the annoying issues of life. When we leave this haven of tranquillity after a weekend, the grandchildren grieve as though a small death had come upon us all. And so it has; they for the loss of this place of wonder, and we for the speed with which they are changing and growing.

This "escape" is from the work of training clergy in clinical pastoral education and doing pastoral counseling in

Southern Baptist Hospital. In addition, Mary Ben and I lead
workshops in family enrichment. In a recent workshop a
lawyer friend, Turner Primrose, said of Mary Ben, "If she
had not said a thing, it would have been worth it just for the
entertainment." This is claiming that Mary Ben is an en-
tirely unique and unpredictable human being. She usually is
her creative self no matter how I would like to put restraints
around her so I can know what's coming next.

We will never be able to pull off the "team" approach
that we see other couples accomplish. It is not uncommon
for us to let the sparks fly in the middle of a workshop. It
wakes up the people. But we don't "stage" such; that would
be worse than staging a picture of perfect harmony and
agreement between two persons.

MYRON

One of the ways that Myron and I have guaranteed that
we will not have a dull life is by having five children. We
have delighted in our family in ways that cannot be expressed. We are aware that having children is not a goal in
itself. Otherwise we would despair when our children become their own persons, make their own life choices. It is
satisfying to feel that we have been a part of a process that
does not stop but continues on a different level as we all
mature.

Growing older in a culture of youth worshipers makes us
look for compensations. Having a family who continues the
process of life, love, marriage is one of the rewards. Having
grandchildren speaks to our need for renewal, affirmation,
the fullness of God's grace.

Myron refers to the fact that we grew up together in a

small Louisiana town. Our parents and grandparents knew
one another and blessed our marriage. It would be natural
to feel that with that background, a good marriage is inevita-
ble. That has been a joy to us, but we have found it necessary
to work at making our life together a good one. We work
at keeping the spirit of romance and adventure alive . . .
though not always in perfect harmony as Myron indicates.

Myron's work has been an exciting, creative, pioneering
effort in the field of pastoral care. He has a unique gift for
being able to identify with a person's life struggles and
enable that person to claim choices for a richer, fuller life.
We have shared in the personal growth process of many
wonderful persons.

People-watching has always been one of my favorite hobbies. I include studying and learning about why we behave
as we do in that term "watching." Myron and I have com-
bined our interest and knowledge in the last few years by
leading workshops and by writing.

MARY BEN

1. Getting to Be Grandparents

LIFE AS ONE PIECE

We live in a time when life tends to fragment between youth and age. If you are above thirty, you are thought to be out of reach of those who are younger. The young separate themselves from the older persons and refuse to identify with them. Perhaps behind all this is the fear of identifying because the obvious message is that when you admit you are a part of the whole human scene, then you admit that you are mortal, given to the limitations of time, pain, and decay.

A prayer of Kierkegaard's brings the ends together between youth and age and relates them to each other:

Oh, Thou that giveth both the beginning and the completion, may Thou early, at the dawn of day, give to the young man the resolution to will one thing. As the day wanes, may Thou give to the old man a renewed remembrance of his first resolution, that the first may be like the last, the last like the first, in possession of a life that has willed only one thing. (Søren Kierkegaard, *Purity of Heart Is to Will One Thing*, tr. by Douglas V. Steere, p. 31; Harper & Row, 1956)

For at least two generations we Americans have lived a denial of age and aging. We have acted as if getting old was the worst thing that could happen to us. The assumptions behind this are:

Old age is to be avoided.

Happiness is to the young.

It's all downhill after thirty.

In other words, we have tended to look at life, not as one piece that we can gather up from infancy to old age but more as a youthful and joyful part attached to a necessary but despised aftermath. It is a sort of reverse of the butterfly where the worm or caterpillar comes first. We might remember the truth in Robert Browning's words:

> Grow old along with me!
> The best is yet to be,
> The last of life, for which the first was made:
> Our times are in his hand
> Who saith "A whole I planned,
> Youth shows but half; trust God: see all,
>   nor be afraid!"

(Robert Browning, "Rabbi Ben Ezra," *The Poems and Plays of Robert Browning,* p. 289; The Modern Library, 1934)

Browning shows an essential continuity and a sense of growth toward age as an enriching process. He saw life as one piece, not a sharp break between the generations.

Proverbs affirms a different focus between youth and age, but this does not indicate cleavage:

> The glory of young men is their strength:
> And the beauty of old men is the gray head.
>   (Prov. 20:29)

The Bible speaks to the continuity and the unity of the individual with the generations in lifting up the common faith of Abraham, Isaac, and Jacob. These three generations of the patriarchs are imaged as having a single goal and purpose.

RESISTANCE

If we have resisted the direction and flow of life from youth to age, we may resist becoming grandparents. This is a special mark of "passage," hence it will give us a truth we may not be prepared to face. This may take the form of preventing the grandchildren from calling us "grand" parents.

The resistance may take the expression of grief or depression, since the fact of becoming a grandparent speaks plainly to the issue of aging. To have a grandchild says all of a sudden that we have moved up a whole generation. We may not have asked to become grandparents, but when it happens, we cannot ignore the reality of it, we must respond.

More often our resistance takes the form of humor. We laugh so we don't have to show our tears. We tease and joke or we jostle one another until the pain subsides, and this is O.K. One reaction is that of getting into silliness.

Still another form of resistance can be denial expressed in acting more youthful. A man might turn to Grecian Formula; a woman, to more sexy dresses. The extreme of this denial could result in an affair for either or both just to prove prowess, strength, and desirability. It all could be saying, "Hey, look, we aren't really getting any older."

FACING UP TO GRANDPARENTHOOD

To be sure, there will be resistance and denial at becoming grandparents. In spite of that negative process, there is a powerfully positive side. The child makes it easy and sets us back on the track of the true value of what life is about. More of that later.

While we usually become grandparents without our choosing, we still have a choice to make. That choice is whether we will go with the process of aging or whether we will resist and deny. In denying, we take grandparenthood as a "fate" imposed upon us. In choosing to affirm it, we claim our "destiny" and go with the flow of existence. Our choice may be the big difference between being dragged by fate or being blessed by destiny. In fate we go backward because we are looking to the good times in the past; in destiny we take hold and go forward in faith that the Creator who gives us a new life has not run out of ideas.

We are in the clutch of fate when we rely on our own human imagination to produce the novel, or when we think our ideas can match the excitement of the birth of a baby. We are free to affirm our destiny when we choose the grandchild as gift and challenge.

Your first grandchild is largely a challenge to let some things pass. The biggest of all is your youth. It is contradictory to be young and grandparent. To be sure, you might pride yourself for a while on being more youthful than most grandparents. Being a grandparent doesn't say in itself that you are old; it does say that time is passing for you.

Getting older doesn't need to be a curse. If we take the

process as our fate rather than our gift, we grow hardened and brittle of spirit. When we are able to enter into the life and sparkle of a baby, we discover that age can actually glow with beauty and mellowness. In identifying with and loving a little child, we recover much of our own "child of the past." A child opens us to greater wisdom and understanding of life. Small wonder that the infant Jesus, cradled in the arms of the loving Mary, has become the focus of our most festive celebration in the Christian calendar.

Age and Youth Belong Together

In his masterpiece, *The Old Man and the Sea,* Hemingway gives the drama of life joined between an old man and a boy. He lets you know that in truth the old man and the boy are a gift to each other, as nature and spirit intended it should be.

> Because of the boy [Manolin] with whom the old man [Santiago] had fished since Manolin was five years old, the old man was not really alone. (Ernest Hemingway, *The Old Man and the Sea,* p. 53; Charles Scribner's Sons, 1952)

The great Swiss psychologist C. G. Jung says that the "wise old man" was an archetype in most of the cultures of the world.

> In other words the "wise old man" was part of the scenery, an assumed presence (for the woman there was also the chthonic mother). (C. J. Jung, *Psyche and Symbol,* tr. by Cary Baynes and R. F. C. Hull; ed. by Violet S. deLaszlo, pp. 21ff.; Doubleday & Co., 1958)

He adds that this image is being lost in modern culture. As the culture has become more youth-centered it lives in Ponce de Leon's fantasy of a search for the fountain of youth. We tend to scoff at age to the extent that we relegate grandparents to silliness and senility. The old man and the boy get lost from each other and neither has what it takes for "passage." Without the boy the old man doesn't have enough to stir him to remember and rejoice; without the old man the boy loses contact with his true destiny. He may create a false one in fantasy—a life where one never really grows old.

Where youth and age are related in meaning perhaps we see again the fulfillment of the prophet Joel, "Your old men shall dream dreams, your young men shall see visions" (Joel 2:28). My belief is that this takes place where the young and old are interrelated, when grandparents and grandchild come together.

The prophet Zechariah gives the prediction of the blessedness of Jerusalem after the restoration. "Once again shall old men and old women sit in the streets of Jerusalem, each leaning on a stick because of their great age; and the streets of the city shall be full of boys and girls, playing in the streets" (Zech. 8:4–5). Age and Youth blend together in that scene of joy and celebration.

A PERSONAL MEMORY

In early childhood (five or six years of age) I remember my feelings that my grandfather was weighed down with wisdom. I liked to be near him and hear his almost daily pronouncements about the world in general, about politics, religion, or economics. As I look back I realize he had more courage than knowledge. It didn't occur to him to doubt himself, nor to me to doubt his veracity. He was the family oracle. His tone of voice was somber and grave in his prophecies, and I felt good just to be near this fountain of wisdom. It never crossed my mind that my grandfather's forecasts were not perfectly accurate and dependable. Since they were made with gravity and a feeling of certitude, I received them in a trusting and unwavering faith.

In these early experiences, it seemed that my grandfather (and sometimes my grandmother) sort of stood in for God. He was my contact with the "Ancient of Ages." He had been born in Civil War days and that seemed like an eternity ago, hence he stood between God and time for me. This made my existence more secure with this godlike grandfather close by to predict what was coming up or to warn us against any danger or threat. Since he spoke with such certainty about the future, it seemed to me he knew it all. Perhaps the gods have never been nearer since that time.

Out of my assumption that he was all-wise, I sought to be around my grandfather whenever possible. Then one day I got a jolt when he told my mother in my presence that he didn't want me going fishing with him anymore, saying, "The boy asks too many foolish questions." At the same time he permitted my two older brothers the privilege of going with him. This was extremely painful. It was a sort of feeling that he represented the tree of knowledge and now I was forbidden access to that tree—shut out of the garden "before" tasting the fruit.

My story had a fortunate turn at this point. In my grandfather's house there lived Uncle Abe, my grandfather's uncle. Uncle Abe had been blinded by a shell burst in the very closing days of the Civil War. He had come to my grandfather's (along with his widowed sister) to live with the next of kin. Uncle Abe was the family philosopher and had been a sort of guru for my father and his siblings when they were children. The fortunate thing for me was that Uncle Abe was willing to listen to my questions. I'm sure I preferred to ask them of my grandfather, but that option was closed.

All of this is to say that the little child is born to ask Why? Sometimes only the patience of grandparents (or older persons) is equal to this barrage of questions. The persons of age also carried more authority for me than parents. There was a feeling that any boy needed the "wise old man." I had him in Uncle Abe, who showed both kindness and patience.

A City of Refuge

Many children look on the house of grandparents as a place of safety from judgment, especially the judgment of parents. In ancient Israel, Moses ordered the setting up of "cities of refuge"—these were places where a murderer could live in protection from vengeful relatives or vigilante groups. Such cities were established for the protection of the accused to give him immunity until he could stand trial. (Num. 35:6–33.)

The term "city of refuge" is appropriate for many grandparents. This does not imply that grandparents are there to interfere with family discipline, yet their presence tends to argue for patience and mercy. Grandchildren know grandparents to be merciful and forgiving in ways parents seem unable. I recall, when the punishment seemed harsh from my parents, a desire to flee to the city of refuge, or the house of my grandparents as a place of mercy and reprieve. There I wouldn't have to bear the burden of judgment and the sting of the peach-tree switch. My word to my mother was, "I'm going up to 'the house' and never coming back." "The house" was the home of my grandparents; it was the big house on the hill that had stood as a place of permanence against change and turbulence.

The house of grandparents is also a needed fantasy for children as a place where they can hide until tempers abate and love returns to cool the passions and quiet the impatient feelings of angry parents. Children under these swirling feelings of judgment need to be able to see themselves in a court of appeal where there is a better chance of having some mercy and grace. They do not need to run, in fact, to the grandparents, but they need the security in the feelings that they are there and that they are loving and nonjudgmental. When judgment is heavy in one place, children need the image of a place where they are not cast out completely and grandparents can serve this need. This is not farfetched from the gospel reality that somehow, in spite of our guilt and failures, there is an abundance of love somewhere to give us the assurance of the presence of a love that is stronger than judgment. The place grandparents live need not be the big house, the mansion, or the four-bedroom apartment. It becomes a piece of glory in the mind of the little boy or girl as long as love is there, given with gentleness. Hence it can be either a spacious place or a single room so long as youth can be stirred to some visions and age can be permitted some dreams.

Roots

Grandparents represent to the child, both the spiritual and the historical heritage, or "roots." The grandfather or grandmother will tell the family "story" of which the child is an essential part, or maybe a central character. This makes the child belong to history, not just to the temporary and fluctuating scene.

Every family has a story, and each child needs the special help of grandparents to tell the story, and to help get the child into the family setting. This is done in particular as a grandmother can tell the child something special and good about his or her birth. This is what Eric Berne calls the "myth of your birth."

In addition to one's birth a grandmother might be the person to tell the child the family history. Every family has its past that becomes essential for understanding its present. The child needs to hear about the past happy times and the family experience of pain and losses in order to get in touch with the flow of family feelings.

Every family has its past sorrows that it carries. Sometimes these sorrows are resolved, sometimes they are not. There are embarrassments, things of shame, and some parts of the story are held in secret. No family is without its share of alcoholics, poor, extravagant, or wasteful members. Then there are records of illness of all sorts, both physical and mental. There are the family winners and the family losers. The winners we tell about in picture and words so very easily. We are tempted not to include the shadow side of the story. Yet a truly faithful grandparent will take the Bible model of telling the whole story of its heroes such as King David who became both adulterer and murderer. The biblical writers didn't touch up the story to make David a saint before presenting him to posterity.

Children don't need to have the older family relatives painted with halos or given white hats. They do better to have the truth as we know it. Only the truth will bless. We don't have to defend Uncle Jasper's weakness for gambling or Aunt Lucy's dependence on drugs. Every family has its con artists, those who don't pay their debts and others who can't keep a job. In addition to this, the family story is incomplete without a record of the natural disasters that occur over a period of two to four generations. Grandparents can nearly always tell of one big flood or fire (or both) and a few hard winters as well as hot and dry summers. Children need to hear all these things as a part of the family story. All of this is valuable material for launching the child toward his or her own story. It helps a child shape life toward a single goal and purpose so that the child may more easily choose a particular direction.

2. Gifts to Each Other

How the Child Is a Gift to the Grandparent

When you have your first grandchild, you suddenly must move into the awareness that you are a generation older. Perhaps you remember how old you thought your grandparents were, and you know you are not as old as you thought they were; at least you don't feel that old. The fact is you don't feel any older at all.

Some people become grandparents before they are forty, others after sixty or later. In any event, when you take on the role, you tend to feel that the clock has passed high noon for you. Usually you are in the afternoon of life. To hold to the image of the clock, most of us are around two o'clock in the afternoon when we take on this experience that can bring unbelievable renewal and sparkle.

Margaret Mead, America's foremost anthropologist, said that it was her grandmother's religious understanding of "who then is neighbor unto him?" that helped make sense out of her concern for the human race. (Margaret Mead, *Blackberry Winter*, p. 3; Simon & Schuster, A Touchstone Book, 1972.)

You had grandparents. Perhaps you recall how you were a gift to them. Having a grandchild binds you to the generations and makes you ask new questions of your faith and your own religious heritage. It may also open new ways of pondering your future and that of the race.

You may be ready to take on the new role or you may not. Ready or not, when it comes you may find yourself rejoicing over the arrival of a grandchild and at the same time you may be resentful, reluctant, or sorrowful that you have been pushed into this new role. The baby does it to you but doesn't at all realize or even respond to the changes this is calling on you to make.

Margaret Mead says it well: "The birth of a child, an extraordinarily small and fragile creature, changes one's own place in the world and that of every member of the family in ways that cannot be completely foreseen." (Margaret Mead, "On Becoming a Grandmother," *Redbook*, July 1970, p. 70.)

You must change in terms of both the past and the future. A grandchild opens the doors to your past as you remember your own grandparents. Perhaps you recall the one you knew and liked best, the one you vowed you would take as a model. It has been many years since you made that vow, but now you feel the need to look back on that model in order to cope with the present.

Your future is challenged also in terms of carrying out your vow: to put into practice good grandparenting ideas. Up to this point it has been a fiction, a possibility, maybe a wish. The birth of a grandchild says that you have no option about being a grandparent. The only option left is a matter of what kind of grandparent you will be. (See Chapter 3.)

The child is your gift. It turns you into a different channel or it helps you steer a little different course. He or she gets you out of the "idea" that one day you will be a grandparent to: now you are a grandparent! You don't learn how to be a grandparent by dreaming about it or even in planning for the experience. You learn when it happens to you. Of course we nearly always want to be the ideal grandparent, yet the particular circumstances usually keep that from happening. As a result, we do what we are able to do rather than what we had dreamed or vowed we would do.

To illustrate: there may be feelings of rivalry coming from the other grandparents. There could be unresolved feelings in your son or daughter that prevent unrestrained celebration or a generous show of affection. There may be hidden factors that leave you puzzled with questions about your own worth or about what rightful place you have in this significant event.

You come to the event of the birth of your first grandchild with a set of expectations or even plans about observing and celebrating it. These plans could hit a snag because of feelings mentioned above. There could be other plans already formulated that negate your plans. This could be very painful, but it can make you aware that as grandparent you are not first in the plans, arrangements, and observances. This is not a repeat of the birth of your first child where you were in charge.

You can make the birth of your first grandchild a great gift, but this may require flexibility and a willingness to take only the leftovers. It is a gift of growth and maturity if you are able to be flexible and adaptable to the various pressures and crosscurrents of feelings that pour forth at this time.

The birth of your first grandchild may be a special gift in calling you to look at human values from which we all tend to stray. Before the birth we get anxious as we did with our own children regarding the health and normality of the child, the safety of the child's mother. Most of us would give at least half of what we own, if, in giving it, we could guarantee that all would go well in the delivery. Since we cannot get any guarantee by pledging our earthly earnings, we at least come away realizing that material value is a poor second to physical and mental soundness.

How the Grandparent Is a Gift to the Child

In the first months of life, the grandparent is not likely to be a special gift except in an indirect way; at least that is how it usually happens. An indirect gift means that the grandparent does what he or she can, to increase the stability and comfort of the environment, working chiefly through the child's parents.

Where grandparents are duly sensitive, they will not offer or push what the parents cannot handle in their feelings. For example, your oldest son has a child while he may already feel too obligated to parents. In such a situation, grandparents will do well to back off and wait, maybe keep a very low profile for as long as the situation demands. These feelings of obligation could build up in the daughter-in-law, and this could put relations on ice for a while.

Grandparents who know how to back off when circumstances warrant are truly a gift.

Grandparents who work to stabilize the environment for the child are showing the maturity that is often needed. They are of special help when they can be available but not pushy, on call but not always present, helpful but not obvious. Since the birth of the first baby doubles the work of a woman's household, good grandmothering offers an opportunity to lighten some of this uncommon load. Yet, it is really no help if it is offered in competition with another grandmother, or if in any way it has strings attached so that obligation builds.

How does one give freely? Sometimes you can't; especially if you offer where another can't receive freely. It is better neither to offer nor to give if the one on the receiving end feels indebted. I stress that it is better not to offer if it is your guess that your gift can't be received freely. If you offer what another is compelled to reject, this results in bad feelings on both sides. Nobody wants to add this to the setting of a newborn infant. The child will inevitably pick up the negative currents and somehow feel the frustration or anxiety in the atmosphere.

The capacity to be aware of the undue pressures in the home of a new baby is a first step toward being able to give a real gift. If you are aware, you can avoid trespassing on territory that is not yours. Your son or daughter may need you, but it is good if you can pick up the subtle signs that tell you just how much or how little you are needed, and when and where you are needed.

You are a gift if you can restrain yourself from being competitive with the parents or in being demonstrative to their embarrassment. Your "being" may be much more needed than your "doing" or it may be the other way around. Your awareness is the key to which is right.

There are some significant factors that you may need to observe, for example, your relationship to your own child and his or her mate. If it is strained in any way, the coming of a child doesn't automatically give the right to ignore past history of feelings. Such things will still need to be resolved, otherwise the little child may wind up paying in some hidden way for past conflict.

Where you live geographically in relation to your grandchild can be a factor. For example, if you live some distance and your own personal needs are cast upon the family with a new baby, you may overtax the facilities of the home. This is usually more a problem for grandfathers than grandmothers since grandmothers are more adept at taking care of household needs. On the positive side here, you may be a little more free in demonstrating your joy and celebration because you will celebrate while taking care not to get in the way; not to stay too long.

Where there are other grandparents involved, it is needful for you to make allowances for their feelings. They have the same rights and claims in the situation. Where they are granted more access than you are granted, it may be a test of your maturity to let it happen.

Another way your maturity is tested is in your ability to be available in the proper ways. Herman Vollmer cautions that grandparents, and especially grandmothers, are sometimes tempted to overstep the proper boundaries. He says: "The ideal grandmother keeps to her own circle as well as in that of her children and grandchildren. . . . She holds herself free of resentment and preserves a suitable aloofness with both child and grandchild." (Herman N. Vollmer,

M.D., "Grandmother: Problem in Child-Rearing," *American Journal of Orthopsychiatry*, July 1973, p. 381.)

Your own position in social and financial matters as well as community status all have a bearing on your ability to draw the proper limits. If you are well endowed in these gifts, it is wise not to overplay your hand nor to become too demonstrative in what you can afford. If you are poorly equipped in the matter of money and social esteem, you don't need to back off in intimidation and fear of rejection. After all, you have given the child a significant part of his or her endowment in terms of the physical inheritance. That is more important than all other resources—whether they be much or little. Things cannot be given in exchange for the life.

If, then, you are in plenty or in poverty, what matters is that you prepare to be yourself in relation to your grandchild. Your knowledge, your experience, coupled with tenderness and care, are treasures that vastly surpass all financial resources when it comes to meeting the needs of a child. It is more blessed for the child to belong than to own. After all, the child possesses the whole creation in the beginning years, and your opportunity is one of being teacher of the truth you have in such a way that you whet the child's appetite for truth in its entirety.

There will be time aplenty for the child to get into the "games" of adult life. What is needed from the grandparent is a guaranteed respite from the undue anxieties and pressures of adult experience so that the eternity of childhood can be a kind of Garden of Eden. This time does not need to be cut short so that children have to take on adult-type worries.

Yet another way that you can be a gift to your grandchild is your availability to bring forth the family story on the one hand and to give direction and dream on the other. Margaret Mead puts it this way, "The strength that comes from a sense of continuity with the past and hope for the future is sorely needed." (Margaret Mead, "Grandparents as Educators," *The Education Digest,* March 1975, p. 22.)

Leo Tolstoy, speaking as an old man, said that from birth to his fifth year was an eternity, but from the fifth year to his old age was but a step. What a gift to be there from one to five!

As a grandparent, you are not there to stop the flow of time, nor to prevent the child from leaving the garden of innocence and beauty. You are there to witness, to value, to affirm life's indivisible qualities—

the same indivisible qualities of Plato's writings,

the same indivisible qualities of Buddha's struggles,

the same that Jesus was speaking of when he said there is no way to be whole unless we also can recover what it means to be a little child.

We cannot recover the event without being with children.

They are our gift.

We can be a gift as well.

3. Feelings of Being a Grandmother; a Granddaughter

"What does it feel like for you to be a grandparent?" I asked one of my neighbors.

"I've been an artist for forty years," she said. "My grandson has taught me a new way to paint. I always thought I had to set aside a whole day, decide on my subject, study it, get equipment and paints together, then spend the rest of my time—uninterrupted—until my picture was completed.

"My grandson, age four, comes bursting in, exclaims, 'Maw Maw, let's paint a picture!' He works on the background, but tells me what he wants me to paint as the main idea. At Christmas, it was Santa Claus. Sometimes it's monsters. In ten minutes we have completed an entire picture —colorful, exciting—satisfying to both of us."

Another friend, when asked the same question, replied: "I enjoyed my children. I've enjoyed watching them grow up and have their children. All of them are real, caring persons. My daughter's middle child wanted to prepare a special dinner for her mother last Mother's Day. She called me and said, 'I want both my grandmothers present on this happy occasion.' I feel like you have it made when your grand-daughter invites you to dinner for your daughter. We feel like we have a dynasty of two children; seven grandchildren. But after being with them for a while and experiencing their 'busyness,' it's good to be back home to our peace and quiet. God knew what he was doing when he gave children to the young."

A friend who has had photography as a hobby for years does not have to be questioned about his feelings of grand-parenthood. His grandchildren are subjects above and beyond all other subjects for photographs.

"It's like being a mother all over again," was another reply.

"It's all good?" I followed up.

"Well, nothing is all good or all bad," my maid said as we shared cleaning chores. We have had the relationship of having her help me care for our children and home for a number of years. She moved back to the home of her parents after she and her husband separated and she has experienced the close family relationship of having her parents share in the rearing of her daughter. When her daughter grew up, married, and brought four lovely daughters into the world, this grandmother was an integral part of their lives. She has helped nurture them during illness and has rejoiced in their success in school. Her reference "being a mother again" was in love, caring, and support.

Another comment: "I enjoy having my daughter and son-in-law and the children over for a visit, if they don't stay too long. Of course, it takes me a while to put things back in place. You know how I've always loved to keep things in order. Seems like children are rougher than they used to be."

A grandfather speaks to grandparenting: "We have to get acquainted all over again with our grandchildren when we go to see them. Fifteen hundred miles is a long way to drive to see our son's family. His wife makes it clear that our presence is an inconvenience, so that hurts us. We find North Dakota cold all the way around."

Another answer: "If you'd asked me three years ago what I thought about being a grandparent, I would have given you a glowing report. Now that my three children have gone through divorces and there has been so much pain and hurt, I don't know just what to say."

A young grandfather told me: "I had just had it with parenting three females when our children got grown. I was not going to get back into that bit with grandchildren. When our first granddaughter came along, I decided that it would be up to her whether she would make a place for herself in my heart. Believe me, she did. I'm hooked again."

SPECIAL PROBLEMS

The life-styles of two grandmothers of my acquaintance are comments on handling a unique problem that many persons must face in our society—that of a retarded child.

As a mother of a beautiful daughter, one woman devoted her early life to planning for and managing much of her daughter's life. The daughter married a successful professional man. They had two children. When a baby, the first son had a serious illness. The grandmother prayed so fervently and earnestly for God to let the child live, she felt that God had spared the child because of her prayers. She took to herself the responsibility for the child's survival. He was retarded. Rearing him as her own, she deprived him of sibling relationships, problem-solving skills in adjustment, special schooling that his parents could well have provided. As time passed, the daughter died; the grandfather who had shared this effort died. The grandmother's life turned into a nightmare of danger and abuse from a huge, hostile, belligerent, frustrated child-adult.

Another grandmother who had a retarded grandchild shows by the beauty of her countenance that she finds great pleasure in being a resource person for her daughter's family. The mother calls upon her for care, support, and affection on a regular basis. Her stance is one of complete love and acceptance, but the child is not confused about direction or obligation.

Another grandmother: "One of the things I like best about being a grandmother is that I can initiate compliments about our grandchildren. I would never have thought of doing that with our own children. Since grandparents are expected to do it, I can brag!"

Still another: "I worry about my grandchildren as much as I did my children. I find I can't do a thing about that. Sometimes my tongue gets sore from having to bite it to keep from saying things I might regret later."

The feelings that we experience in having a grandchild take us back to our own experiences of being a grandchild. We tend to recall expressions, cautions, even little songs and family sayings that contribute to our image of what a grandparent should be like.

MY MOTHER'S PARENTS

I felt warmth and joy in my maternal grandparents' house. Some of the recollections of my granny's kitchen are: hot biscuits baked in a wood-burning stove, rich cream gravy, home-cured ham and bacon, eggs laid by proud cackling hens, boiled ears of corn pulled in the garden minutes before they were placed on the platter. Granny's "plain" cake was a tradition at church dinners and community gatherings. I cannot duplicate the fineness of texture using my electric mixer. I remember how she sat in the kitchen chair and beat the batter until it was light and fluffy, then turned it into a well-buttered pan.

"I just burn one stick of stove wood at a time," she told us to indicate temperature control.

Summertime was the season for filling rows and rows of jars with fruits and vegetables against the winter. Sugarcane was taken to the syrup mills and converted into ribbon-cane syrup. A pitcher of this golden brown delicacy was always in the center of a large, round table to be poured over biscuits buttered with freshly churned butter. Granddaddy always grew enough cane so that when the grandchildren visited, they could make taffy. We boiled the syrup until it was thick, pulled it into light-colored ropes, placed it on marble where it hardened. To add to the festivity, there was corn to pop and peanuts to parch.

At dinner and supper the bread was made from cornmeal, buttermilk, and eggs. The vegetables that have come to be called "soul food" were a regular part of the diet.

My mother's parents had ten children. There always

seemed to be enough food and enough room for family and guests who happened in for a stay—long or short. Guests were welcome for the "pleasure of your company." Family members, hopefully, contributed by sharing the work load of the farm. This home was a retreat when the children were "between jobs," "down on their luck," or, as we say of our children today "finding themselves."

I remember standing on a chair to wind the handle of the Victrola in the living room. My young aunts suffered me to play their records which I recall broke quite easily. I learned to do the Charleston from them—a dance which, I modestly admit, I still do rather well. This activity was not exactly encouraged. In fact, it was barely tolerated as our church frowned upon this kind of exercise of joy as frivolous and approaching the margins of sin. I remember Granny's sorrow about her daughters dating young sports who called in roadsters with the top pushed back. They would not return until well past bedtime. Though I appreciated her feelings, I could hardly wait until I got old enough to do the same thing.

Once I remember going to my grandparents' home on a fall afternoon and the backyard was alive with activity. Everyone was bustling around with special jobs to do. I learned that the occasion was that Granny was making lye hominy. I'd observed that she had been saving ashes from the stove, and had stored them in a bin. Somehow the potency was extracted by pouring boiling water through them. This, then, was added to dried, shelled grains of corn. The corn swelled, was rinsed, and then was cooked in a large pot over an open fire until done. Some was eaten fresh, but most of it was stored in jars. Using dry corn in this way was developed during the Civil War when there was so little food in the South. My granny had learned it from her family. I have bought hominy in cans to recapture that taste experience, but nothing has ever come close to that full-bodied, wholesome natural taste.

My mother told me a story about Granny's spunk that I'd like to relate. During the early years of marriage, Granddaddy was a deputy sheriff of his county. He had to be called away on duty one night. Someone came to the home, called for the sheriff, and was told that he was not at home. The caller then proceeded to break the door in and came into the house. Granny grabbed a hot poker from the open fireplace where it was lying in the coals. She was able to defend herself and the little children and drive the intruder away with this most unlikely weapon. My mother was one of her young ones.

As these grandparents grew older, the youngest son, Keller, devoted himself to helping care for them and holding the home together. Finally, with progressive illness, they moved into the homes of daughters who lived nearby. My mother cared for my grandaddy who lived a number of years after Granny died. She modeled a special kind of beauty of spirit and devotion that seems sorely lacking in our modern picture of family relationship.

My mother's parents provided security and retreat for their family. In return, they reaped the reward of love and devotion to the end of their lives.

My Father's Parents

I didn't feel a sense of belonging in my daddy's parents' home. On a typical visit, we would find Grandpa sitting on the porch in a swing, or about the chores of the farm. "Nonnie," as we called grandmother, was usually sitting in the dining room by the fireplace doing some kind of fancy handwork. We visited with each of them separately for a while—I don't remember any laughter.

Daddy felt that the oldest son in the family was my Grandpa's favorite. My daddy resented the partiality and I remember stories of how he felt "put down" as a child, by unfavorable comparison. There were seven children in his family.

I never heard my grandmother call my grandpa anything except "Mr. Gray." Since this formality puzzled me, I remember asking my parents about it. My daddy explained, "That is her way."

My mother's comment on why our visits were brief and uninvolved was, "Children make Nonnie nervous."

Grandparents relate to their grandchildren in a way that feels natural to them. By the time their parenting days are over, they feel as the young grandfather did whom I quoted, "I had just had it with parenting!" Others continue the loving, caring relationship until the end of their days. I feel that I experienced each of these feelings.

4. What Kind of Grandparent Are You?

There are as many different kinds of grandparents as there are persons in the role. Yet there are types that resemble one another. In other words you will, in your own role as a grandparent, be more like some, less like others. Even in the same family a grandfather might be one type, a grandmother a different type.

The way you function as a grandparent is influenced by a number of external factors as well as internal or personal factors. The external and internal factors also interact on one another. Let us look at these things which influence grandparenting and then go on to reflect on some of the types of grandparenting that prevail.

External Factors

One of the chief influences on your function as a grandparent comes out of what you believe is expected of you in the role. There are role stereotypes that are reflected in the media such as grandmother shown as a little white-haired lady who depends on her children and grandchildren to keep her from being lonely. Sometimes the picture is in contrast:

the grandparent holds power and control with either wealth or sickness. Pity and guilt are feelings that some grandparents use to make claims on their grandchildren and children.

In some ethnic groups economic power and prestige rest with the old. Dorian Apple has pointed out that where this is the role model, the relationships between grandparents and their grandchildren are formal and authoritarian. (Dorian Apple, "The Social Structure of Grandparenthood," *American Anthropologist,* Vol. 58, Aug. 1956, pp. 656–663.) It could be that this is your own background and philosophy.

You will be in a majority on the American scene if you are one of those grandparents who is more removed from family authority and you are expected to enjoy some sort of equalitarian or indulgent relationship with your grandchildren. (Bernice L. Neugarten and Karol K. Weinstein, "The Changing American Grandparent," *Journal of Marriage and the Family,* Vol. 26, May 1964, pp. 199–204.) Peter Townsend has called this "privileged disrespect" among the English. By this he means that grandparents and grandchildren tend to overlook the age and "respect" factor and find a common ground of mutual enjoyment in spite of all the differences.

In addition to what your culture places on you as an expectation about grandparenting, there are such added things as your occupation, your commitment and relationships to friends, your hobbies, the relationship to your children, the number of grandchildren you have, your age, and where you live. Some of these are outside your ability to change; others may be subject to your choice and decisions.

They all have a direct bearing on how you perform as a grandparent.

For example, you are a young grandmother, you work, you are involved in church and social life, and your grandchildren live several hundred miles from you. Under such circumstances you may not choose to be regularly involved with your grandchildren. At least you are not yet the little white-haired lady waiting for a telephone call from them every morning while you are having your coffee.

Internal Factors

There are things that relate to you as a person. The kind of person you are says much about who you are as a grandparent. You have lived much of your life becoming a grandparent; now you will keep on being yourself (we hope) and expressing who you are in your relationship to your grandchildren. We will reflect on some of these.

Emotions. How do you handle your emotions? Do people think of you as open or closed? Warm or distant? Look at emotions another way. Do you suppress your feelings tightly, or do you find meaningful ways to express them? To be more specific, what do you do with your anger? Can you be straight about your anger when someone frustrates you? I mean by that, can you say you are unhappy about being put down or ignored when you really are unhappy about it? Please don't hear me telling you to get into shouting or stomping matches in your anger. You may do just as well to swallow it.

It is good to be able to do what Jesus said here, "Let your

'Yes' be 'Yes,' and your 'No,' 'No' " (Matt. 5:37). This could simply mean that it is not good to turn a no into a yes just to be the nice guy. You will pay for that in headaches, upset stomach, high blood pressure, and the like.

If you have difficulty being honest with your peers about your feelings, then you will tend to take it out on mates, children, and puppies. Your grandchildren will learn from you what one is to do with strong feelings. You may "teach" them proper ways with words, but they will learn from you by the way you act.

Possessions. This could be simply a repeat of the last point because people handle their money as they handle their feelings. If you are open with your love, you will likely be open in your giving things of a tangible nature.

People whose emotions are blocked so that they don't give much love and warmth will usually keep a tight fist on their purse strings. It is not only true that "where your treasure is, there will your heart be also," but as your love flows, so flows your cash.

This is not a suggestion that you turn into a free spender as a grandparent to show some love. It is important, however, that you be yourself. It is also important to do as Socrates said—"Know yourself."

Time. If you would be a good grandparent, you might need to learn from your grandchildren how to get lost in time. Do you remember how a fifteen-minute recess in elementary school was sufficient for a round of baseball or basketball? When a child asks for some of your time and you have only fifteen minutes to spare, that might be enough—

if you really give it. Victor Hugo said that becoming a grandfather was "stepping back into the dawn."

I have already affirmed that we are all different, yet we have many areas in which we are alike. It is these common areas to which we will give our attention. I have limited this to what I consider four types of grandparenting. They are (1) the party type, (2) the authoritarian type, (3) the reserved type, and (4) the holiday type.

The Party Type. This is the kind of grandparent who is a liberating spirit, one who can get into the precincts of childhood with a sense of frolic and fun. It is what Neugarten and Weinstein call a "fun seeker" ("The Changing American Grandparent," p. 202). This is largely the kind of grandmother that flooded the childhood of Margaret Mead and helped her stay youthful all her years.

The party type of grandparent is the one who excites and stimulates the child with both "fantasy and festivity," to use Harvey Cox's phrase. This helps the child start the process of assimilating two conflicting worlds that always press upon him or her: the world of nature (what "is") and the world of culture (the "ought"). Nature is the world of mood and feeling; culture is the world of control over the raw stuff of nature.

The child who has a "wise old man (or woman)" as a role model will more comfortably bring together the paradoxes that keep coming up between nature and culture. The pressures between these spheres are enough to fragment life for the child. A grandparent becomes a ready-made assurance that one can survive in spite of the conflict. Then to add to the scene, a grandparent who can enter the "party" is a living example of what biblical faith is about (Karl Olsson). We may need to remind ourselves of this when we fall into thinking that Christianity is a set of rules. It is more about loving and celebrating—and becoming as little children.

The Authoritarian Type. This is a second style of grand-parenting. Margaret Mead's grandmother was more this type even though paradoxically at times she was all fun and frolic. In fact "grandma" was the essence of authority, as related by her granddaughter:

> My mother was trustworthy in all matters that concerned our care. Grandma was trustworthy in quite a different way. She meant exactly what she said, always. . . . She simply commanded respect and obedience by her complete expectation that she would be obeyed. (Margaret Mead, *Blackberry Winter*, p. 45)

Because of your ethnic background, or a rural upbringing, or perhaps your own personal makeup, you just might be the authoritarian type of grandparent. I am not putting that down, and I am not urging you to change to a type that does not suit you as a person. If you are the authoritarian type, you can meet vital needs in your grandchildren—more by being yourself than in any other way.

The authoritarian grandparent more often takes responsibility to be the "chronicle" and the "oracle" in the family —saying from whence we came and predicting whither we are bound. This was my grandfather as noted in Chapter 1.

That grandparent tells the "story" weaving the threads of family life into those of community and hence the nation. This helps the overall sense of belonging to take place. It is what Alex Haley has done for black people in *Roots*. It is especially good for children to know they are in the flow of the stream of history. That flow needs to comprehend and merge the stream of nature with that of culture.

The authoritarian grandparent is more akin to what Neugarten and Weinstein call the "reservoir of family wisdom" style of grandparenting ("The Changing American Grandparent," p. 202). Where more attention is given to a reflection of the past, these are the grandparents that go more by the book of expectation out of the past. This is not saying that you are without spontaneity, yet spontaneous behavior may be less a part of grandparenting here.

The Reserved Type. The third is the reserved type. Perhaps you can say whether you are this type by going back and asking how your feelings flow (or don't). If you are a reserved person who does not come with balloons and sparklers on every occasion, and you are not set in a mold of authority in the family, this does not negate your right and ability to be who you are to your grandchildren.

Grandchildren can be a special blessing to you because they have that wonderful gift of being able to accept you and love you as you are. You, in turn, can be just as great a gift to them if you love and accept them as they are without pressuring them to be different. Parents are caught up in a strong need to change their children. In changing the child, they are often trying to refine out traits they despise in themselves. While you don't have to discourage that process, can you show patience with it? Your children are practicing on their children what you taught them a generation ago. Forgive yourself by showing patience and acceptance by just being there as a grandparent.

The Holiday Type. This type of grandparent I would describe as one who, in the normal course of things, is involved in his or her own life, vacation, hobbies, friends, etc. This grandparent marks off time for grandchildren on special days. This may also be dictated by the fact that you live some good distance apart.

Families that live apart may get together only at holiday times. This may be the only occasion for being with your grandchildren. You may at these times have a good chance to relate. It can still be very special for you and your grandchildren to look forward to these times. Between times you can build up your plans about what you will do next holiday. It could be a fishing trip, a ball game, or just the sharing of a special book or story. The child might want some reflections about his or her parents when they were children.

Christmas is usually the big holiday for giving gifts, but birthdays can be even more special between you and your grandchild. This calls for planning and thinking ahead so that you can give something of yourself on birthdays. If you cannot be present on the birthday, you can write a letter. A letter is ten times more effective than a phone call, though calls are special too. But a letter shows your thoughtfulness in ways a phone message fails to do. To rephrase the idea —to *be present* is best, but if that is not possible, *send a present that reflects yourself.*

Children enjoy ritual. You may be thinking what new and

different thing you can do each holiday or birthday and the children may be disappointed that you didn't do what you did last year. After children do a thing once or twice they tend to say, "We always do so and so." They cherish the familiar feeling.

In conclusion, I would like to illustrate grandparenting that encompasses all the "types" mentioned. You may be a grandparent who moves about on the scale from one polarity to another. Certainly there are times when you are in the party mood and other times when you are not.

The illustration is a tender story of a grandfather in Robert N. Butler's Pulitzer Prize-winning book on aging. He says in the introduction of this grandfather:

> I remember his blue overalls, his lined face and abundant white hair. He was my close friend and my teacher. Together we rose at four A.M. each day to feed chickens, candle eggs, grow oats, and tend to the sick chickens in the "hospital" at one end of the chicken house. (Robert N. Butler, *Why Survive? Being Old in America*, p. ix; Harper & Row, 1975)

A grandfather who could turn one end of the chicken house into a hospital was giving the foundation for a seven-year-old boy to become a medical doctor; and an author who wrote with due appreciation of the grandparents of America.

It is good to be encouraged as a grandparent, to know you can be a part of the treasury of memories in your grandchildren as long as they live. Margaret Mead so treasures grandparenthood that I would like to share her words:

> The closest friends I have made all through life have been people who also grew up close to a loved and loving grand-

mother or grandfather. (Margaret Mead, *Blackberry Winter*, p. 56)

If your grandparenting has results as its purpose, you may miss its greatest rewards. Grandparenting is for entering again into childhood—to reenter "fantasy and festivity" and to "step back into the dawn."

5. The Inner Life of a Child

The purpose of this chapter is to elaborate something of the inner world of the child: the first five years of a child's pilgrimage as a little human. It is written to make you more aware of the value of this time of life; perhaps to recall some of it. It is not written to frighten you into walking on eggshells for fear you will make some fatal mistake that will distort the child's future.

So much has been said about these impressionable years that we often get the mistaken notion that what we do "determines" the child's later years. To be sure, these are shaping years, but there is a difference between experiences that shape and those which determine. It is a kind of fatalism to think of persons being determined by their environment. Humans have choices to make all their lives. There is freedom for you and for your grandchild. We will consider these first five years in stages.

THE FIRST YEAR: A PERIOD OF GRACE

You might look on the first year of life as a sort of year of pure grace. You can call it that because the world around the child is traditionally set to give to the child's every need and wish, while at the same time there are very few if any real demands imposed. It is a year of giving on the part of adults and a time of receiving for the child.

At birth the child is open to multiple stimulation pouring in from the environment. Before birth the child is protected from most such stimulation. The birth experience is usually a painful one, not only for the mother but for the child. He or she issues from the womb through the narrow squeeze of the birth canal, and this hurts because of the pressure on all sides. The child usually comes into the world with swollen eyes and cheeks, with a narrowing of the cranium from this prolonged time of getting out of the prenatal place of comfort and even luxury.

The baby leaves all this inner security within the mother's body for a space that could be anxiety-producing simply because it is so wide open, so unguarded, and so radically different. The womb was kept at a constant temperature, while the room may be hot or cold or the temperature may fluctuate. The womb was fluid and smooth, the sheets may be rough, and they are surrounded by air, not fluid. There are raucous noises, voices, coughs, rattling of instruments, sounds of television sets, and all the usual business of a hospital.

The child is transported now by one person or another with different touch and perhaps cold hands. These different hands come attached to strange people who don't have the same rhythm as the mother or the same care. He or she must keep eyes closed much of the time because the eyes have never been exposed to light, which irritates and annoys.

In addition to the multiple stimulation coming from the outside, there is a reversal of the body function so that air must be taken into the lungs. The stomach cavorts, the intestines are peristaltic; the food can bring pain and pleasure. From inside and outside it is all a strange and new experience. This is not implying that the child is self-conscious about how strange or different all of this is. However, he or she may be protesting it with a cry. The child is being dragged into something for his or her own good, but the feelings may not be saying that one feels good about all of this. Certainly we have no way to communicate that all will be well.

The new infant comes into life with practically no defenses against this exterior environment that we have described as one that bombards the child with stimulation from every quarter. These stimuli are not all unpleasant, some of them are no doubt enjoyable. But the chief point of stimulation develops around the process of nursing, at least the most pleasurable is there. The lips and mouth become the point of contact with the mother which the child has lost in the physical separation at birth. Whereas the two had been one in prenatal existence, they become one as a functional unit in postnatal life.

As a part of nursing, the mouth of the baby becomes the chief body zone of pleasure—an "erogenous zone." Undue frustrations in the first year of life tend to interrupt the natural fulfillment and personal growth that come in nursing. Psychologists go so far as to call this time the "oral period" of life because of the intense focus on feeding as being center stage during the first year. They also point to the fact that if a child goes through this period with minimum satisfaction between himself or herself and the mother, that child will in adult life tend to reach back in some form of regression just to complete these earlier frustrated needs.

Certainly there are experiences that show how the first year of life can carry over into later life. For example, if a child is delivered after the amniotic fluid is lost (called a dry birth), there will be crawling sensations of the skin in all of life thereafter. Again if the stomach valve is blocked at birth so that food does not reach the stomach (it may take a few days to diagnose and make surgical correction), one will be a voracious eater for years thereafter. It is as if one counters the early starvation experience with the aftermath of perpetual hunger.

What is most important in the first year is a happy and caring mother; one who is free to put the child's needs on the highest priority list. The mother is not just a source of food, but of loving care if she is going to have a happy and growing child.

Anxiety in the mother introduces a strange factor in the baby's life, and the baby is not equipped by nature to deal with anxiety. A mother's anxiety does not necessarily get into her milk to disturb the baby's digestion, but she can communicate it by the change of body rhythm, the shrill voice, the absence of tenderness, or in whatever avenue the baby receives stimulation from her.

A grandparent will be a useful person if he or she is able

to minister in some way to the needs of an anxious mother during this time of caring for an infant. There are literally dozens of things that can make the mother anxious and many of them are valid. Some of them may be within your capacity to change, others will be outside your reach. It is good to know where you can and where you can't help. You lower anxiety if you act in a proper time and way; you increase it if you become pushy in ways that add to the mother's burden.

About the best you can do is to ask yourself what all the needs that may be going unmet are or what fears and apprehensions may be present. You may offer to do what you are able, or you may ask if there is anything you can do—if you really mean that.

We have given a heavy focus on food and feeding in the first year. It is true that food is important throughout the life-span. The child equates being fed with being loved. It is as if he or she said, "If you love me, feed me; if you feed me, love me."

A tragic feature of the early months of infant life is called the marasmus condition that babies develop when there is not sufficient bonding between mother and child at the start. When this happens the child turns away from the mother and the feeding process and literally goes on a hunger strike. This will lead to certain death unless it gets special attention so that the child is given the appropriate love and care to stimulate again the desire to live.

A grandmother sometimes becomes the chief source of care and love for a baby, but this is not the usual case. More often she is a backup source, and that is vitally important.

The first year, then, is characterized as a time of pleasure, of receiving, responding, being loved and cared for. Demands are not often made, limits are not set, and discipline is to come later.

The Second Year: A Time of Limits, A Time of Expansion

If you stay with religious language, this is the time when the child learns the "law," or "thou shalt nots." This is all for a reason. The child is learning now to have some self-control through learning to use his or her own muscles to walk and manipulate arms and hands. We encourage development and movement, but there must be restraints. The walking gets our praise, but it must not be in the street. One must not touch the stove or the electrical outlets.

There are literally dozens of cautions that we issue regarding knives, scissors, and pins. Perhaps the child feels that we adults are always saying "No, no." He or she learns well to say it back!

Another part of the second year is the child's development of control over the contents of bowel and bladder. This may give him or her the first awareness of the power to control something that no one can touch except by the child's permission. An anxious mother may attempt to force the child to comply with her needs in the matter of toilet training. The child is relatively free to comply or to assert some rebellion against compliance.

A very intelligent child will easily discover that he or she has come into a position to "bargain" for the first time. Such a child may exploit that position for whatever power might be gotten. Whereas the mother had loved freely before, she now may say she will love if the child will observe the proper rules in controlling feces and urine and in depositing these in the appointed places at appointed times.

A child may come through this experience with the assumption that one must perform properly if one is to be loved. She hears the words, "Mama loves a clean girl." The implication is that she doesn't love a dirty girl. Perhaps this is the origin of: "Cleanliness is next to godliness."

A grandmother is not there to do the toilet training, nor to see that the child is always spotless. Neither is she there as a witness to the beginning of life, namely, the original experience that love and grace are present no matter what.

A nine-year-old girl, answering, "What is a grandmother?" said: "A grandmother is a lady who has no children of her own. She likes other people's little girls and boys." (*Guideposts*, May 1977, p. 21. Quoted from Dr. James C. Dobson, *What Wives Wish Their Husbands Knew About Women;* Tyndale House Publishers, 1975.) When grandmothers do this, they are not relaxing the rules that are painful for children to learn, they are providing the grace it takes to accept some of the limits they must accept in order to complete the socializing process. This socializing process is a necessary part of preparing the child to live in a world of people. This all begins in the second year with a "no, no."

In addition to our setting limits upon the child in the second year, this also comes as a time for the child to expand his or her own boundaries. This is the glorious time when children learn to talk and walk.

In his second year, our youngest grandchild, William, would come with us to the country occasionally. He was spellbound by butterflies, lizards, crickets, turtles, fireflies, and the many varieties of life not seen in the city. His routine was to come up on one of these surprises in nature and say, "What is it, Pipe?" (Pipe being what he called me). I would answer by giving the name of whatever he asked. He would pause, look amused, ponder a bit, give out a tiny laugh of seeming appreciation for having mastered another section of the universe. Then he would pronounce the name of this new creature. That also was an occasion of mutual laughter. I came away from each such venture with William with a feeling of kinship with Adam, who had the privilege of naming everything in the first place. I sort of had the feeling that William would have given each creature a name if I had not been there to give the common name.

It was too early for him to ask the use, the purpose, or function of these various life forms. He gave off pure delight in having them named. It was as if he was in touch with the deeper meaning of the introduction to John's Gospel when John wrote: "In the beginning was the Word." For a child, words carry power.

The child is coming into power when he or she begins to use the proper word. Grandparents have a unique opportunity if they are called on by a grandchild to teach some new words.

Another area of expansion for the child in this period is that of learning to walk. Mary Ben and I remember with such delight how William would, on first getting up in the country, spread his arms and trudge across the dew-laden grass as if he meant to rise up to the treetops to meet the sunrise. He had to go to meet all that outdoor wonder as soon as he could keep his balance enough to drink it in.

THE THIRD TO THE FIFTH YEAR:
FINDING AN IDENTITY

In the first two years the child has consciousness of other, of surroundings, of pain, of love, of food, etc. There comes a time when the child moves from saying "me" to saying "I," from being object to being subject.

A little four-year-old girl was feeding a duck in the park. It was her first experience with such a creature. She asked what it was and her father told her it was a duck. Her question then was, "Does he know he's a duck?"

There are many things perhaps that ducks know, but they don't know that they know. This is where truly human existence becomes possible, where we know that we know, where we ask the question of who we are.

Children divide the human race into two parts—mamas and daddys, or female and male. Our grandchildren, Sara and Gray, four and five, will be in a room with a group of people of all ages and about the first thing they do is report how many "boys" and how many "girls" are present.

Grandparents need to be aware of the fact that little boys first get their identity from the father or the most available male. If they can't get it from the father, the grandfather is the one to whom they may look to get it. Little girls likewise identify with their mothers first and grandmothers second.

In addition to the identification with the father, the little boy looks to his mother as the one to love him. He gives more admiration to father, more love to mother. The little girl identifies with her mother, is more loving toward her father, and yet has to depend on her mother for her care and most of her love. That is usually because the mother is more available to meet these needs.

When you add this up for grandparents, it is important that you do what you can to strengthen the bond between your child and the mate. Little children's needs are better met when the bonding between their parents is secure and firm. The marriage bond needs to come ahead of all others.

An example: A son had his first child and went to his mother to confide in her some of the difficulties he was having in his marriage. The mother heard her son, but she held her tongue and gave no advice. She didn't take her son's "side," she just listened. In not taking sides the grandmother was left free to be a grandmother, whereas if she had sympathized with her son, the emotions could have been jelled against the daughter-in-law so that grandmothering could have been resisted in some way. Sympathy cast on the son's side could also have led to an erosion of the marriage bond.

The child needs the freedom to explore who he or she is in terms of both sexes—a mother and a father. Many are able to find their identity under more limited resources, but why not give the best we are able? In one-parent homes, grandparents can help greatly as male or female models.

The third to the fifth year just might be the best years of grandmothering. These are times when the questions come. Such questions as these can't be answered: "Why isn't God married?" or "Why does God let people die?" or "Why can't there be girl daddies?" Maybe the reason children need grandparents is that they can hear such questions without a put-down or a laugh.

These are the years of honest quest, of Why? The child really wants an answer. He or she is asking what your assumptions are, and if you truly listen, you will ask yourself again if you have forgotten to keep asking your own questions. Where was it you started giving answers rather than putting the question?

For most children these are the years when they learn about "limits" in a real way. In the second year the limits are the man-made sort, the rule, the "no, no." In the fourth and fifth years the child learns about *time,* a limit imposed from the outside.

Time is a measuring device for people. It says where they get into life and where they get out. Time says there is a real limit imposed from the outside in terms of a beginning and an end of human existence. The child in this period needs a grandparent who will hear the pain and uncertainty in dealing with beginning and end—birth and death— "Where did I come from and where am I going?" and why? He or she needs to get beyond, "The stork brought you and angels will take you." The only consistency in that answer is that the dirty work is done by feathered creatures.

The child resists having his or her little eternity broken or watching Humpty Dumpty get shattered. Perhaps the Humpty Dumpty story is the nursery-rhyme version of Adam in the Garden of Eden. At any rate, the joy and beauty of being a grandparent in this period is one of preparing the children, like Adam, to live somewhere east of Eden or outside the garden.

6. The Outer Life of a Child

THE VENTURE OUTWARD

Just as life in the womb is radically different from postnatal life, so life centered in the family for five years is different from life outside the family. When the child starts to kindergarten, he or she is not expected to leave home, except for a few hours at a time. But school is the beginning crack of a final break somewhere down the stretch of time.

The break from home is done, as already indicated, a few hours at a time. Kindergarten is a sort of practice run to begin a process that is meant to end in full separation and relative independence for the person. The child who slips and falters in this process is usually pushed along or forced to keep up the pace even when the feelings are not cooperating.

An example: A graduate student came for counseling who couldn't get through a single semester without a couple of trips home when this was costing him more than he could afford. In addition, his wife was losing patience with this routine. He went on to tell his story. As a child he lived adjacent to the school grounds where he attended grammar school. He was an only child. His parents were divorced when he was in the second grade. At that time he developed a panicky feeling and would run across the school grounds to his home before school was out. He said he never stayed at school a full day in elementary school; he just couldn't do it.

After telling his story he was able to see his pattern and said: "I seem to be doing the same thing in graduate school." He was still running home to mother by catching a plane every month or so and flying across two states.

Grandparents as a Safety Factor

In the above case the grandparents were missing; they lived in distant places and the child was all that a bereft mother had for consolation. He probably went home as much to meet her needs as to meet his own. Once this pattern was established, it was very difficult to change. It is a pattern that possibly would have been averted had there been the presence and support of grandparents.

It is easy for parents to lose sight of long-range goals when they get caught in divorce, grief, financial reverses, job loss, etc. These things invariably make it more difficult for children to keep on reaching "out." From anxiety and safety needs they tend to regress and hold on more tightly to the ever-dwindling patch of their security (Abraham Maslow). This in turn may make the parent more anxious, which creates still more anxiety in the children.

There is a kind of psychological law at work: Children can venture out in direct proportion to the safety and security they feel behind them. In other words, children can face up to new experiences if things are nailed down behind them. No combat unit can do battle if it gets cut off from its supply lines.

Grandparents are a great source as backers, encouragers, supporters. They can be a valuable asset in stabilizing the mood and atmosphere around the children so that a venture out is not felt as such a high risk. You can't hope to take all the risk away, but maybe enough to make it tolerable for the children.

SPENDING THE NIGHT AWAY

A small child's growth comes in being able to separate from parents by going in the daylight hours to kindergarten and school. Another step of growth comes in spending the night away from home. That often is a very big event, and it is made easier when it can happen in the home of grandparents. Grandparents are usually able to provide the loving security around the child that is almost equal to the security he or she feels at home.

Children who never spend the night away from home tend to have greater difficulty with homesickness when they make this step in late adolescence such as occurs when they start to college or go away from home to work or for military experience.

Being away from home only in daylight hours is not enough to shore up the child's confidence about being able to cope away from the parents. The experience of spending the night away from home is of value in helping the child depend on an alternative set of emotional resources. He or she may need to know that survival is possible should anything happen to the parents. Sleeping away from home for a night or so at a time tends to fortify a growth toward self-sufficiency that few things can give a child. Very often grandparents can serve this function by providing the necessary familiarity and support.

The house of a grandmother at nighttime can provide additional things for a small child in the time of establishing identity and separation. It can be the opportunity to give feelings of uniqueness and specialness. You may need to take into account the child's need for this when there is extra stress on the child such as the birth of a new sibling or the time for an older sibling to leave home. This can be at any time of shock, trauma, or loss. Much can be gained if the child can change scenery and get a generous supply of care and love. It could be a time when you simply provide an ear and answer questions as best you are able.

When Parents Hold On Tightly

Sometimes parents forget the object of helping their child reach increasing independence. They get anxious or they grow sentimental or they are simply lonely. This can lead to their clutching and clinging in the very times the child may be reaching out. As a grandparent you might come to the rescue if you see what is happening. You can be an anchor or a help to offer a needed support in some crisis, disappointment, or failure.

I am not so much speaking of a readiness to bail your children out of some financial crisis as I am thinking of the power of emotional support and encouragement when there is failure or fear of failure. One of the strongest temptations is that of giving financial support if the crisis is financial. You might guard against giving support that will have to be offered over and over to the degree that it becomes crippling.

There is sometimes a parallel struggle going on: Your son or daughter attempts to gain financial freedom from you while their son or daughter attempts to gain emotional freedom from parents. The ties between parents and children may show much dependency for more than a generation. Yet the natural flow toward relative independence is expressed by the three-year-old child saying, "I want to do it myself, Mama." Perhaps all our lives we feel the urge to be totally independent on the one hand and on the other to have the security we once felt as little children in the shelter of our parents, grandparents, and siblings.

As a grandparent you can never be totally free, if that means being completely independent from your children and grandchildren. Your lives are interwoven, interlaced, and bound up in a common heritage. Sometimes you want distance from each other just to have more personal autonomy or feelings of independence. At other times you will seek more closeness to remove the fear of isolation and abandonment.

Parents are constantly in the above struggle with their children; children feel it with parents. The place of the grandparent is one of observing the fluctuation without alarm. It is all right if your grandchild moves up and down the scale from being independent to a return of more dependence on his parents. It is getting to be a common pattern for children to return home after a year or more away. If they return, they might be seeking what was missing earlier in the home setting. They might be in need of special attention and care even in their twenties or later.

The place for grandparents in the above struggle is to remain in a neutral corner. It can be very easy for you to take sides: *with* the grandchildren under usual circumstances of their pushing for growth and distance; *against* them when they rebel to the extreme.

GAINING AUTONOMY

Your grandchild can bother you from two sides: First, you may see that the child is too cautious and fears to risk new relationships. Second, you may develop concern that he or she cares so little about family that almost any person is preferred over the parents as models.

In the first situation the child cannot seem to turn loose from the family and the past; in the second he or she may be rejecting everything that has to do with the family. Neither of these is a healthy outlook. Grandparents cannot always bring about the miracle of change, but your loving presence will be a corrective influence. You need to remember that the parents usually push in the first situation to get the child to stir about more. In the second instance they likely are doing the opposite: holding back, pleading or arguing for behavior change.

Of course, as a grandparent you also want to get some changes going, but could you take a different approach? Could you avoid getting hooked into a program of lecturing or pointing out faults? Can you accept that the child has chosen his or her pattern? This is in fact a truth. Let it be understood that you accept the choice to be one way or the other.

Persons do not make serious behavior changes until they decide that they can reverse some bad choices. They are unable to do that well until they become aware that they are where they are because of their own choices.

Parents and grandparents cannot make the decisions that lead to personal autonomy for the young person. *Decisions make people grow and people who grow make decisions.* Growth comes in learning how to separate and how and when to unite. Persons need both closeness and distance.

7. A Sense of Belonging

Providing a sense of family history is one of the things that grandparents are able to do for a grandchild. Myron refers to this and I would like to talk about some things that we have worked on.

During the terminal illness of my mother, I took many of the family pictures and mounted them on poster board so that Mother could look at them and remember the joy of other days. After Daddy died and the household was broken up, I brought these and many other pictures home to preserve, sort out, and arrange in some sequence of order. Several years passed before that could be done. Finally, when Myron was away for a week and the children were "on their own," I dedicated time to carrying out the resolve to "do something about those family pictures!" Since this was a lifetime investment, I bought the best-quality albums available. I sorted out what seemed like bushels of pictures by person, relationship to family/friends. From the pictures of our five children I made a collage of each child—from birth to the present.

At that time, the frames with mats precut to insert pictures behind were not readily available; so the artistic results were more crude, but the fun of displaying and viewing the pictures was rewarding. Some enlarged pictures such as high school graduation, plays, special vacation events were put in frames and hung on a single wall which has become a panorama of Madden family history. This collection of pictures has grown and changed through the years as children marry, grandchildren arrive.

The grandchildren look at and talk about their parents, aunts, uncles, and themselves and observe the physical growth and change of these persons so important to them. They compare their looks with family members at the same age.

These pictures give children a sense of time, growth, and development in a frame of reference that is a part of their experience.

Children enjoy having stories told to them about themselves—how they looked and acted as babies. Little incidents about themselves make a special event of any quiet time together. They also enjoy being told about their parents' childhood—which can include toys that they played with, a trip to the hospital, the birth of a new baby in the family, a special Christmas. These stories help the grandchild realize that Daddy and Mother were not always adults but can identify with him or her because they, too, were children.

Grandparents can sometimes have the patience and creativeness to teach a lesson by telling a story rather than getting into the parent stance of "should" and "ought." As a child, I remember breaking a measuring tape that my daddy valued very highly because it was "indestructible." I felt a real challenge to try my strength against it. Instead of fussing at me, he told me a story that involved respect of property and ownership which I remember to this day.

Once in a workshop we asked our group to draw stick figures of four persons who were influential as their parenting models. They named the relationship of the figures, then listed six adjectives that would describe that person. As they looked at this background of authority figures, we hoped that they would get in touch with their own parenting techniques which came from these models.

A lady came to me privately and told me that one of the strongest persons in her background was her grandmother. Because her parents had separated it had been necessary for the grandmother to live in the home with the mother and children. Since the mother worked to support the family, the grandmother had taken over the mother role of the family.

"I hated my grandmother and do to this day. I cannot resolve my hostile feelings toward her yet. In listing her characteristics I find that she has the qualities that I most admire and she is the person I would most like to copy as a parent for my children." Since there was no follow-up on that brief moment of intimacy, I can only hope that with the insight that came, she can make peace with the memory of her grandmother.

As we look at our own relationships, what are the traditions of our family? What can we do to pass on a feeling of continuity? of belonging?

Some of the answers lie in:
    being together;
    not watching television together,
        but talking to each other;

being present to each other;
being aware of feelings—
　　feelings where the joy is,
　　feelings where the hurt is;
exchanging ideas about the past, the future.

There is enough divisiveness from outside. Families need to feel a bond of:

togetherness,
affirmation,
strength,
continuity.

Grandparents have the privilege of representing this bond. They can portray the past with affirmation, the future with hope.

8. Relating to Young Grandchildren

GIFTS OF SERVICES

It is a common concept that grandparents enjoy "spoiling" their grandchildren with gifts. Usually this gives good feelings to grandparents and grandchildren alike. Yet Myron refers to the fact that under some circumstances perhaps this kind of generosity may cause bad feelings for parents, resentment from other grandparents. Sometimes gifts other than "things" are a more acceptable expression of love. To borrow a term from the economists, we can think in terms of giving "services." A very satisfactory gift that I have never heard criticized is an agreement of certain times when grandparents will be available to keep children. This gives parents a few hours to use as they need. I suggest a specified time to be agreed upon so that misunderstanding will not develop. The gift might be, "I'll keep the children every Tuesday from three thirty until nine o'clock for two months." At the end of that time an evaluation can be made and a "renegotiation" can take place. This does sound businesslike and formal for a family relationship, but this will keep down feelings of "being imposed upon," or "being

71

taken for granted." The main idea is to keep communication open.

If parents live a distance from their sons or daughters, providing money for domestic help during a crisis time might be acceptable. Or if grandmother doesn't work, she may go herself to "help out" during illness, birth of a new baby.

In our situation, because our daughter has been in law school since the birth of her son, she and I have worked out a new "contract" every semester. I keep him at different times according to her need. We look forward with great joy to our time together. One semester she had an eight o'clock class. Myron's day had the happy beginning of having our grandbaby arrive while we were having our coffee on Tuesday and Thursday.

I have acquired a collection of toys for the grandchildren, some "previously owned," from garage sales. These toys provide an immediate feeling of warmth and familiarity from visit to visit.

LONG-DISTANCE CONTACT

Staying in touch with grandchildren and claiming a place in their feelings is a challenge when parents live a distance away. Writing letters can be a help. As a six-year-old, I lived with my maternal grandparents when my parents made a job change. I needed to complete the school year before moving. My daddy wrote letters that he printed in bold alphabet; he drew cartoonlike pictures for some characters. One story was about buying a new pair of boots. He drew a picture of his old boots with a large hole in the sole. Years later, when the picture of Adlai Stevenson was shown with his foot propped so that a large hole in his shoe was a focal point, I got in touch with good feelings from that letter of my childhood. Telephone conversations can do just what Bell Telephone advertises that they will do, "Keep in touch."

The investment in a tape recorder by parents and grandparents enables tape letters to be sent back and forth through the mail at minimal expense. Think what a library of memories this can provide!

Our oldest son, Mike, lives four hours away. The occasion of a visit is such a time of celebration that I have had little arrival gifts for Sara and Gray. Leaving time was sad—so I came to realize that a departing gift is more appropriate, so now I give each child a little package as they get into the car to leave. This takes tears out of separation and occupies some of their traveling time.

CHILDREN AS PERSONS

Eric Berne made the concept popular that each person has three ego states: parent, adult, child. It helps, sometimes, to remember that a child, too, has these ego states. As mood, the child flows from one ego state to another according to what seems appropriate at the time.

Our two-year-old grandson, William, and I were walking up the stairs. Each of us was holding a glass of Coke. I hated to remark about his tilted glass but was thinking about the possibility of a soiled carpet when he glanced at his glass, looked at me and cautioned, "Be careful, Mimi, don't spill it!" He had learned my parenting lines.

Since our grandchildren are young, the relationship is

primarily a nurturing, loving, caring one. Yet I try to listen to their thoughts about school, their friends. I try to be alone with them so that we can relate as persons to each other. One of the favorite things that we do is ride the streetcar from our stop to Canal Street, then back. Since Sara and Gray are first year in school now, their observations and interests are very different on this trip from when they were younger. On our last trip, Sara—with pencil and paper— kept a record of all the persons who got on and off the streetcar.

Myron speaks of the time after two as being the time when we put demands on children to conform to the ways of society. We parenting persons begin the "shoulds" and "oughts." This is a time when children become aware of power. The fantasy of this time is "monsters"—a terrible power from without that could destroy them. We use information and techniques to control and "train" children. They, on the other hand, are feeling this and trying to survive. The children, too, are learning something about control, so we get "no, no!" temper tantrums. They realize that one of their areas of control is toilet training. It is during this time that they begin to get into their feelings of self-worth. More about that a little later.

I mentioned the ego states in children. It has been interesting to observe this at work in our grandchildren. Someone mentioned that in order to learn about the child ego, we should observe a child. Five-year-old Sara is a year older than Gray. Usually their interaction is creative, happy, typical child's play—talking, make-believe, sharing. As toddlers, Sara tended to dominate the relationship. At times she would act like a parent by scolding Gray; at other times she would love and nurture him as if he were much younger. By the time Gray was three years old, I was interested to notice that he had become aware of what was happening. He showed his claim for power in the adult role in a game they played. He made a train out of chairs, and told Sara where she should sit on the train. She protested, but he was firm in his plan. He would not take her ticket until she observed his rules. He was, of course, the conductor and the engineer. Sara had mixed emotions about this change in dominant behavior by her brother. This power struggle is interesting to watch during our visits.

Children learn about how to behave and adjust by the feelings they get from their parents and other authority figures. "Be quiet," "Be still," "Go watch TV," "Don't bother me," give children the feeling that the important people in their lives would be happier if they weren't a part of the relationship. The children's very being is not important. Giving time, listening, answering questions, stroking a child are a contribution that grandparents can make for the children. This can add to what parents do in terms of teaching how to be close and warm in a relationship. From a practical stance we must admit that it is not always possible to be all that we hold ideal in a given situation; we do not always feel like rising to the occasion of complete patience, complete frankness, warmth, and love. Being straight, explaining, "I don't feel like doing that now," "Will you wait until another time?" "Can we talk about that tomorrow?" are concepts that feel logical to a child—yet do not feel like a put-down.

Children get too few unconditional strokes for *being*. This is where grandparents can make a real contribution to a child's strength. Grandparents are in a position to affirm in an understanding way. Parents must feed, support, school, train, "civilize" their children, and take the harassment of getting on with their own life. Grandparents, we hope, have gotten through a good portion of this struggle, in terms of home mortgage, career achievement. Grandparents can relate in a way that makes the grandchild feel good about being a member of the family.

What Will They Call Me?

The importance of naming comes out in the feelings of grandparents in expecting a first grandchild. In talking to persons about their feelings of identity, we ask about the meaning of the name—first and last.

Who gave you the name? What feelings go with the association of the name? What do your peers say about the name? Does it feel like a joy or a responsibility to carry?

Anticipating a first grandchild, we think, What will the child call me? I remember a conversation with a beautiful grandmother in her seventies who was telling me about her grown grandchildren. She said with such disdain, "They always called me 'Granny.'" I could feel her resentment that a name had been put on her that she was not ready to cope with as a younger woman. It was not her choice of an endearing name.

Usually grandparents are in a bargaining position in terms of what the baby will call them. This is important because the term is something we carry for the length of our life. Once I asked one of my friends who was blessed with grandchildren before my grandmothering days, "What do your grandchildren call you?" It seemed like a logical question at the time. When she replied that she did not know, I was mildly shocked. She was with her oldest son's children a great deal and very much into her grandmother role. I pondered the fact that she possibly had confused her role with that of "mother," but I did not feel free to press the issue.

Sometimes grandchildren will get into the pattern of calling a grandparent a special pet name of their own, for example, William, our daughter's child, has been fascinated by the fact that Myron smokes a pipe in the evenings. He calls Myron "Pipe." His French grandfather is "Pa-pere."

While our son's children call us "Mona and Granddaddy" and our daughter's son calls us "Mimi and Pipe," it is interesting to note that when they get together, they work on getting the name and identity straight.

What's in a name? Usually whatever our grandchildren call us sounds like real love when it comes from the lips of our grandchildren.

9. Middlescence–Adolescence

Children reach adolescence about the time their parents reach middlescence. Both ages present identity problems. Parents are evaluating their feelings about career, home relationships, their future, and what they have become. Adolescent children are looking at the same problems from the opposite time frame. Both evaluations are strongly influenced by peer relationships.

Parents are comparing their success, failure, accumulation of wealth, achievement of influence with their friends. They are reflecting on their expectation of life and measuring it against what they have accomplished.

Teenagers are looking at their expectations of life with hopes and dreams and misgivings. Often family stress develops at this time because of lack of communication.

In adolescence, such a dramatic change takes place in the physical and psychological makeup that young persons feel that they are experiencing a unique phenomenon. Nobody else would understand. Often they have inadequate information to interpret this change.

Some adolescent thoughts:

> Does anyone else have feelings like this?
> Why do I feel terrible one minute and great the next?
> Why do my parents have to be so dumb?
> Will they ever learn?
> When will I start growing? or
> When will I stop growing?
> Am I some kind of a weirdo?
> How can I get the guy or gal in school to notice me?
> Will my skin ever clear up?
> What am I going to do in life?

Middlescent thoughts are something like this:

> Am I as much of a man (woman) as I was?
> Should I be thinking about changing jobs?
> Wonder if I ought to see a doctor about this depression I've had lately.
> Maybe I need glasses.
> Should I use a little hair color to cover up this gray?
> This weight has sure slipped up on me!

ADOLESCENT REBELLION

As children begin to rebel at the rules and regulations that have been a part of their training, parents feel anxious about their authority. This rebellion feels scary.

Some of the facts of our present condition make this fear

justified. We don't have precedents for solving these problems.

1. Affluence makes it possible for children to move out of the home and into an apartment at an early age.
2. Readily available "wheels" provide mobility and anonymity.
3. Popular acceptance of freedom in drugs and sex challenges our past values.
4. Upheaval in the structure of society regarding race puts us in a situation of rethinking our pride and prejudice.
5. Situational ethics as a moral standard puts a strain on traditional attitudes of right and wrong.

PERMISSION IS THE KEY

What part can grandparents have in coping with these problems? Grandparents have to accept the fact that they can relate to the situation only as they are given *permission*. If the relationship of grace, love, maturity can be maintained, grandparents can do a great deal.

Permission is the key—from our own children—from grandchildren. Being aware of permission requires intimacy of relationship which takes into account *real feelings!* Each person in the relationship must be respected as an individual. For true intimacy, one needs to be able to listen with the heart as well as the ears. The right to make judgment, give advice, or make suggestions does not necessarily come with the territory. It feels to grandparents as though it "should" because that is our background.

We began this chapter with the thoughts that parents and teenagers are getting new feelings about their identity.

If parents have not worked through their identity regarding who they are, career stability, marriage relationship, etc., it is important for grandparents to realize that their own sons and daughters may regard the relationship with their parents as one of their problems. Myron speaks to this in the section, "When Parents Hold On Tightly," in Chapter 6. They may be reexamining the parental ties. In counseling middle-aged persons, we often find some who are struggling with feelings of being tightly bound to parents. This shows up a strong drive to please parents, a need to be in constant touch, a struggle for feelings of self-affirmation and self-worth. Though these middle-aged parents have children of their own, they still are unable to be peers with their parents. In cases where parents are struggling with relationships with their own parents and are also trying to cope with the need of their children, they find themselves in an emotional double bind. The process can be helped when grandparents become aware of this struggle, and can allow room for growth and show patience and understanding.

Sometimes these growth and identity crises produce so much hostility in the home that children seek a refuge of warmth and acceptance elsewhere. Myron's oldest brother made his home in the "big house" of grandparents for a time for this reason. Grandparents can be a strength and resource to their sons and daughters as well as to their grandchildren. Providing a nonjudgmental attitude where feelings can be aired, perspectives put into focus, can be a contribution of a grandparent's home. Affirmation of persons as individuals is important at this time. Keeping a low profile on issues but affirming individual worth can keep the struggle from developing into a win-lose situation. In a family struggle, if one person loses, everyone loses. Grandparents can help deal with feelings by: (1) accentuating the positive, (2) pointing out that now is not forever, (3) reminding children and grandchildren that feelings change. The wisdom of experience and age can provide support and nurture.

FEELINGS OF RESPONSIBILITY

One of the reasons that grandparents can maintain a "cooler" posture is that public opinion does not hold them responsible for the behavior of grandchildren. Whether children will be debit or credit to their parents is an anxious responsibility. Parents who regard their children as an extension of themselves feel great pain when children begin to rebel at parental control. Even parents who regard their children as "individuals held in trust" sometimes feel threatened by their children's growth and maturity. It feels as though the structure of the family home is being shaken. It is easy to forget that the family unit must self-destruct so that children can begin their own lives, their own homes. In our book *The Time of Your Life*, we discussed the fact that it is sad when children leave home. But it is sometimes sadder when they do not. Children need to be motivated to get into their individual process of growth and development.

What has this to do with grandparents? When sons and daughters and grandchildren give permission, grandparents can be a great natural resource. They can affirm both generations to continue their maturing process of developing their gifts and talents. They can be available to supply understanding, hope, warmth, affection. And most importantly— grandparents can provide *relationship!*

10. Grandparenting for Puberty

For some of you, grandparenting is phasing out when children reach puberty. For others, it may only be beginning. This all depends on the total array of circumstances. Hence, as in all grandparenting, you may need to give much or little.

THE PARADOX OF HUMAN GROWTH

A human being grows by venturing out and returning. Growth is defeated if one ventures out beyond the capacity to return to the self. The image of baseball is appropriate. The object is to knock the ball as far as you can and go around the bases and back home. When you touch home plate you are back where you started, but the score has gone up.

If you are in mid-life or later, you probably have had many experiences like the baseball game. No matter how far out you venture, the game of life is lost if you are not able to relate it to the point of beginning. Schizophrenia or the split personality is that situation where one has ventured too far out and is unable to relate present experiences to past experiences—to tie life up in one package—"to will one thing."

83

The paradox is lifted up in the fact that big problems arise when persons venture too far out from the self, yet even greater ones arise from that person who musters no venture at all. This is seen in the typical hypochondriac who is so bound up in himself that even the least move outward is done only with great effort. Paul Tillich says, "Going out from one's self and returning to one's self characterizes life under all dimensions." (David Belgum, ed., *Religion and Medicine*, "The Meaning of Health," p. 4; Iowa State University Press, 1967.)

We have already talked about this need to venture in Chapter 6. If you, as a grandparent, were able to nurture the process, it only becomes a natural step for you to continue that support in the puberty experience and beyond.

THE PUBERTY CRISES

You are better prepared for whatever role you play if you realize that the onset of puberty often puts a family in stress like few other perils of family life. The stresses take various expressions. We will now consider some of them.

Financial. Children coming to puberty exact more from their parents than earlier. They require and expect better clothes, more spending money, more time with their friends, which means more entertainment and food outside the home.

In addition to all the above, they require and often demand room or space in the house that affords more privacy. This may strain family budgets to add a bedroom or an extra bathroom or both. In many cases this will call for a move to a more expensive house and into a more expensive neighborhood.

Pressure may also build to have more adequate or more expensive automobiles. Children this age often select the most affluent peer in school or church as the ideal model for dress, transportation, and entertainment. I often pass a large high school as parents are dropping their teenagers off in the mornings. It is not uncommon to observe those in less than new cars stopping a block or so away from school to let children out. Those riding in the new and expensive models are more inclined to unload nearer the front entrance. The same pattern holds for the parking of vehicles. The more conspicuously expensive the auto, the nearer to the campus it tends to find its day's lodging. The rattletraps and junk cars seldom appear front and center.

Emotional. In addition to extra financial pressures that children exert at puberty, there are many emotional pressures. Grandparents do well to be aware, whether or not they are able to make helpful suggestions or changes.

At this time there is more conflict in the person at puberty—internal conflict. This conflict is felt in the relationships to parents. For example, a son may easily get his mother's sympathy in all his struggles. She may take his side and support his wishes without realizing that she has not brought her husband fully into all that she feels. This can result in greater marital disharmony.

A child entering puberty brings as much stress on the relation between parents as any event in the history of the marriage. If, for example, the father handles conflict by withdrawing, he may cop out by taking on a second job. In this fashion he can rationalize his generosity toward the family by pointing to his long working hours. Yet the hardcore truth may be that he prefers to work longer hours in order to avoid conflict with his teenage son or daughter. He may, when all is said and done, be making virtue out of necessity.

Grandparents are seldom in a position to "do" anything once they observe the heightened conflict between teenage grandchildren and their parents. You simply become a source of sanity when you refuse to ring the fire alarm over these spats, quarrels, and threats which come into focus.

Social. For the young person at puberty, the greatest driving force is often a search for peer blessing or at least a nod of approval from the leaders of the peer group. Again you cannot change this fact as a grandparent. You can just make it more bearable if you know what is going on.

One of the really difficult issues is the fact that parents tend not to accept the friends their children make. Let me illustrate:

A couple came for counseling with the stated problem that they could no longer cope with the fact that their children kept bringing home such unacceptable friends.

These parents had always rejected their children's friends. Their children were sons, twenty and eighteen, and daughters, fifteen and twelve. The point of conflict was the constant fighting about the friends that the older sons brought home.

I asked to see the sons together with the parents. It turned out that the sons were not able to make friends with the cream of the school and neighborhood. They were "average" and their parents were about the same.

I then asked the parents if they might possibly find some way to accept their sons' friends in spite of all the past hassle. They did and the atmosphere of the home took a turn toward peace. The sons began a program of striving to be helpful about the house.

Grandparents are a valuable resource in just accepting whoever and whatever comes along. Parents are caught more in the struggle to climb and to succeed while the unshaven, unkept friends of their children threaten the image. A grandparent in the neutral corner again can be a stabilizing influence.

Sexual. You need to be aware of the sexual struggles of the human being who is coming into physical maturity before developing the proper skills for relationship. As a grandparent you can provide a quiet place for grandson or granddaughter. You can listen and you can care; you don't have to coach, advise, teach, or preach.

Teenagers have anxieties about venturing out, about exposing their thoughts or their feelings. They are afraid to share, and they are afraid not to share. They get mixed up, confused, depressed, and again they explode with laughter and happiness. On a given day a granddaughter might be expressing ultimate despair about life, the world, her family, or whatever. The next day might see her explosive with joy as if the whole of creation was in her grasp; this change is possible because the right boy asked her for a date.

Your special gift may be in going with the mood—"rejoicing with those who rejoice, weeping with those who weep."

Sexual guilt is a heavy factor among teenagers. They feel

guilty about their sex feelings and they have guilt and re-morse over any expression or gratification of their drives. Virtually everything associated with sex has the potential of producing guilt. This, very likely, is the one greatest source of guilt in the teen years.

There are not many times that grandparents get the story about sex guilt. It is important that you know that sex guilt is usually there in force. It erupts with the onset of puberty and is usually strong for years thereafter.

Because of the awkwardness and swift body changes of puberty, young persons will often have feelings of *shame* that are much the same as guilt feelings. They don't need any more shame heaped on them from the outside since there is already too much working on the inside.

Identity. As a grandparent you need to model acceptance in spite of awkwardness, timidity, and pimples. You may indulge your grandchildren in memories of happier days, or you may be creative enough to help them project to the future. It is good sometimes to get them away from the feelings of self put-down that often becomes extremely pain-ful. Above all else, you need to show acceptance and care when they are having difficulty liking themselves and claim-ing their own identity.

The early teen years are the times when a young person would abandon being the self in preference to imitating some good model on TV or in the movies. You can permit these fantasies of escape from the self, but your presence can be an invitation to come back to the self to pick up the necessary task of putting life in one piece and giving it direction.

The strength of the Christian faith at this juncture is not that of offering an escape for the young person but of giving a unifying center, one that can be a focus for all the fragments that tempt one to organize life around several centers.

11. Living Together in the Same House

My parents lived with my father's parents until after my oldest brother was born. They lived there while they built their own house. I always had the feeling that the price my mother paid for this was that of allowing my grandparents special rights to her oldest son.

It has amazed me how many times I have seen this parallel with other families—the first child may become a sort of special gift to the grandparents. Then the grandparents, as mine did, may make a special claim upon the first child.

The story of Franklin and Eleanor Roosevelt was one in which the grandparent was in charge since they lived in Mr. Roosevelt's mother's house. When you speculate on the strength of that grandmother you know that you are dealing with the "authoritarian type."

Children after marriage may not openly choose to live with the parents of either mate. Yet it often becomes more convenient or less straining financially to do so. There are many and varied circumstances under which you as a grandparent may find yourself opening your house to your children and grandchildren as a place to live.

I am not discouraging letting your children live with you

even when they have children. It is done very often and for a variety of reasons. The following are some of those reasons.

REASONS FAMILIES LIVE TOGETHER

You have the space and they can't find adequate quarters.

You may be lonely and the thought of waking up to the laughter of children is exciting to you.

You have a house and they can't afford space that is equal to yours.

They need a place to live and you need the extra money they are willing to invest as rent or board.

They need the extra care that grandparents (especially grandmother) can give, and both son and daughter-in-law (or daughter and son-in-law) work outside the home.

Your children need to stay at home in order to complete an education or training process.

They may need you for a recuperation from some illness, with special needs for care of the children.

They might have a child with special needs and they are not emotionally or financially able to carry the burden without some extra help.

Grandparents are often a good resource under these circumstances:

After a divorce your son or daughter might ask to live at home again with their children.

After the death of a spouse, your son or daughter might want to return home with a child or children.

Because of separation due to military service or work overseas a daughter might return to parents with her children on a temporary basis or she might ask to live in the home of her in-laws.

Unusual hardship may make it necessary or more convenient for young families to merge with parents. This could include hurricane, tornado, blizzard, or flood. It might also cover such things as sudden job loss, fire, illness, accident, or some financial reverse.

EMOTIONAL FACTORS IN LIVING TOGETHER

The above examples will suffice to illustrate many of the external forces that explain why children return to the home of their parents. In addition to all the above there are emotional factors to be considered. These have most to do with the fact that the ties are not yet resolved between parent and offspring. This leaves a need for them to live together in order to complete and perhaps finalize the separation process. We might add that living together could help resolve the dependency factor, but it could work in the opposite direction, leaving the child or parent (or both) more, rather than less, dependent.

It is appropriate now to cite some of the features of emotional dependency that foster a longer period of living together on the part of the parent and offspring. The following are examples that I have observed:

A parent (or parents) pushed a son to become independent too early, or at a faster pace than ordinary. This left the son with unfinished needs at home after living away from home some ten years.

Parents prevented a younger child from learning how to take care of himself. They always reminded him that he was "the baby" and couldn't do what the older siblings did. They left him with a willingness to let others look after his needs. He remained at home after marriage and played the helpless role.

A father died, leaving his twelve-year-old son (second child) with a commitment always to take care of his mother. He married with no thought but to bring his wife to live in his mother's home.

A less-favored child returned home by playing on his parents' guilt. He told them how they owed it to him to let him bring his wife and two children to live with them since the parents had done more for an older brother and sister.

A father, not being able to accept his eldest daughter's leaving home, offered the son-in-law a partnership in the business if they would live at home.

A son, not wanting to leave home, made himself so useful in the family business that his terms of staying in the business was the privilege of living with the parents after marriage. This is a very common way that children hold on to the parental nest; they become too useful for the parents to risk getting along without them.

A less-favored daughter took her mother's illness as her opportunity to move her family back to her parent's home so she could better look after her mother. She made no offer to move out once the mother was back on her feet.

As you contemplate the emotional factors, you might speculate that we humans could get sick and have other problems in order to meet our dependent needs. I am not putting that down, but let me add that greater growth usually occurs when we are aware of what we are doing. We need to be aware of our choices; in fact, we need to know just how hungry we get in some of these family areas. We also need to know that because of our feelings we may not be able to look at the facts.

WHERE THE SON OR DAUGHTER HAS THE HOUSE

We have been looking at the situation of two to three generations living together in the house of grandparents, but this is not the only arrangement we see these days. It is possible that you, as a grandparent, find yourself living with one of your children (or with more than one). In other words, you do not own the house but you become a guest in the house of your offspring.

Some of the reasons that bring parents to live in the home of their child (or children) may be a reverse of the reasons given why children return home to live with their parents. The emotional factors stand. They are often a strong and moving force to put families together. We will not list those again because this could be a showing of the same coin from the opposite side. I will proceed now to list some of the situations I have observed that bring parents to live in the homes of their children.

A woman of seventy living alone reminded her daughter on every contact that it was the daughter's duty to take the mother into her home. The mother felt abandoned and alone and thought her ills would be resolved if she could be with her daughter and grandchildren whom she loved. The daughter finally gave in, mostly because of guilt, and asked her mother to move into her house.

A widow woman of forty-seven was almost violent in protesting her daughter's marriage. Immediately following the marriage the mother got sick, moved to her daughter's new home, and remained with the daughter as an arthritis victim. There she lived as a helpless person until her death twenty-nine years later.

A woman of forty lost her mother of sixty-three years of age. In her grief that daughter insisted that her sixty-five-year-old father move in with her and her family even though the father had his own house. This daughter had always longed to give her father the tenderness she felt her mother couldn't give. The move was premature because both daughter and father had not worked through their grief.

A man went to live with his second son in the hopes of stabilizing his son's home. That son had a severe alcohol problem.

A woman moved in with her son and her son's family after her husband died. She lived alone in a distant city in an unsafe neighborhood. There seemed to be no other option.

A woman, a grandmother of fifty-five years of age, went to live with her daughter and three children after the daughter's husband died. The grandmother moved in to take care of the children so the daughter could work and support the family.

The above is a sampling of situations that are fairly typical. Parents live with children and grandchildren in order to meet their own needs or the needs of the younger generation. This depends on where the greater needs are.

No matter where the major need rests, it is usually a good procedure to have a working agreement before you move into your children's home or before you have your children and grandchildren move into your home.

SOME ELEMENTS OF A COMMON UNDERSTANDING

When families merge into the same living space there needs to be some kind of open discussion and agreement ahead of time about many things.

Space itself is important. There should be agreement about how the space of a house or apartment is to be occupied. Each person will need to be accounted for in the space he or she will occupy. This needs to be done with each person present for the discussion and agreement. Space limitations should be agreed upon before the move is made. For example, if two or three children must share the same room, then they need to agree to this ahead of time.

In addition to the regular use of space, there needs to be some agreement about space changes at times when additional persons, such as other relatives, visit in the home. This needs to cover altered sleeping arrangements at those times. There should be an agreement for open discussion when and if a space crunch should exceed the ordinary expectations.

The cleaning of space needs a general agreement, especially the space that is used in common. For example, there will be much traffic in the kitchen. In order to keep down friction, it is good to have an understanding of how the dishes will be kept clean, as well as the floors. What will be the routine for handling the garbage?

Assuming that there is one kitchen and one common pantry, it is better to have an agreement on both the purchase and the preparation of food. Most people have some peculiarity that will annoy others such as a liking of a certain brand of food or drink that he or she wants to keep in a separate place. These things need to be aired as much as possible beforehand or shared when they surface later.

Routines are important as a part of several people living together. Private routines such as time for exercise should give way to family demands. For example, one person shouldn't have the right to do a thirty-minute jogging program while the rest of the family waits supper on him or her. Habits of TV watching should be discussed. Space for children studying should be separate from the TV area or if there is no such space, there should be agreement to sacrifice television in favor of some good reading program while children study.

Where two families merge in the same space and time, you may want to work out holidays and other times for being apart, going other places, or doing different things. If you are a grandparent with other grandchildren, you might develop a plan to see them regularly.

Weekends need an understanding and agreement beforehand. Most families use time on weekends for recreation, worship, and maintaining house and yard. The common tasks that are spent in upkeep need to have mutual participation and sharing. It is not proper for one person to mow the yard every Saturday if other able-bodied family members spend the same time at the beach or the park. As nearly as possible, the regular weekend chores need to be named and portioned out by common agreement.

Budget matters should not be assumed or kept secret. Since such things as food and fuel are common expenses, there needs to be an agreement to keep these things out in the open to prevent a buildup of feelings such as may occur when one person is spending more than his proportionate share. This sort of thing often leads to conflict. Sometimes the real cause of conflict is hidden or suppressed and it becomes more difficult to resolve. These might be peculiarities, habits, and idiosyncratic behavior, which are all a part of living together. There needs to be a common understanding about the smokers as well as the snorers. There may be late sleepers and early risers, free spenders and misers, drinkers and teetotalers. All of this needs to be faced in the open with each person who is subject to annoyance or inconvenience having input. This is not to imply that things can be worked out so there is no conflict. But frustration can be reduced greatly when people are willing to discuss their mutual problems in a spirit of concern and care.

When it becomes necessary or appropriate for families to live together, it is important that the agreements be entered in a positive spirit of a common opportunity. Human beings don't have to be defeated by some common misfortune if that is what brings them together. This can just as well be the opportunity for people who love each other to find mutual ways to grow and be happy together.

Any agreement you make should be open for negotiation, since living together will produce the needed experience that may call for change. It is a good practice to establish an agreement to bring everything up for further consideration after a month, three months, or six months.

12. When Grandparents Become Parents

Dealing with Feelings

Many people at mid-life (or later) are drafted from being grandparents to being parents to their grandchildren. This happens in various ways, but more often at the death of one or both parents of the children or on the occasion of divorce.

If you are in such a position, you may need to deal with your feelings. Those feelings will likely be a mixture of good and bad.

The feelings may start with the grief that makes the move necessary. You may also be angry, frustrated, or deeply disappointed. You had planned your life in a certain direction and now you must go in another. You may feel exhausted from raising your own children. You had looked forward to getting it done, yet now you must turn around and take on another load.

It is good if you can give yourself a right to whatever feelings you have. It is not insane for you to be delighted and disappointed all in the same day. Children may make you very happy in the moment and may heavily tax you in the long haul.

After raising your own children you have a right to feel hurt or resentment if you fall heir to a second family before you get your second wind. You may need to remember that little children are not the causes; they don't need to get the blame for doing things to you or others. They are there with many needs that cry out to someone to respond.

If you are the one to respond and if you are able to do it, you will have a decision to make. If you take on a child or children as the primary support, then you need to do it out of choice, not out of necessity. But you say that you must do this because these are your grandchildren and everybody expects it of you. You don't play a fair game taking on parenthood if you can't find it in your spirit to do it out of choice. It doesn't matter if all the world votes you into the position. It is unfair to yourself as well as your grandchildren to enter a forced arrangement of parenting them because you feel you can't escape it. There are too many other able and loving people in the world who would like to do what you dread doing. It is O.K. to let them do it.

Another argument surfaces from inside yourself: will others think you are weak or selfish for having questions, negative feelings, and fears? They probably will, but you can't control what others think. Should you let their thoughts control you?

In most circumstances, grandparents move to the role of parents when the need arises. Yet if you must move in this direction, it is wise to talk with others that you respect and let them hear your apprehensions and anxieties. Get the feelings out with friends so you don't have to put them on the children.

EXAMPLES OF HOW IT HAPPENS

There are various circumstances where grandparents are called to move to the role of parenting their grandchildren. Let us look at some of these situations.

A daughter has a baby out of marriage and wants her parents to take the child and rear it so she can finish her schooling and get on with her life. Parents usually assume that they have no other option except to take the baby as their own child. This is not a fair assumption. When you consider the number of people who are young and vigorous that want a baby, you may need to rethink your own age, strength, finances, and health. If any of these are not in proper order, you may want your daughter to consider adoption outside the family. What is most important is that you give due consideration to the baby's needs, not your own wishes. If, however, you as grandparent take on the role of parents, you will want to assume all the privileges as well as rights. This will include proper adoption procedure.

Grandparents come into the parenting role when both parents are lost by either death or desertion.

A daughter moves back home after divorce from her husband. She brings her children and continues to be the mother. However, without a father, the grandfather moves to a parent position while the grandmother continues the same role. The reverse may occur when a son loses his wife and returns with his children to his parental home. His father remains the grandfather while his mother moves from the grandmother role to a mother role.

A grandparent may be drafted into a parental position

because of illness. For example, a woman with children gets tuberculosis making it necessary for her to be hospitalized while her parents care for the children.

In other situations, grandparents may become responsible for the care of grandchildren because of the mental illness of a son or daughter who had custody of the children.

Not an unusual case of grandparents taking over a child (or children) occurs when a son, for example, has the custody of children that he can't for some reason continue to give his care and support.

A son may ask his parents to take his children because he plans to marry a woman with children and he prefers not to attempt merging two families of teenagers.

Establishing Agreements and Guidelines

The above are examples of the fact that grandparents are often thrust into the responsibility of assuming a parent role for their grandchildren. When this occurs there are a few important guidelines that may help in coping with this kind of responsibility. The following are worthy of consideration:

Establish Lines of Authority. If you must act as parent, then make sure you have the authority to do so. Have this understanding all the way around.

Have an Understanding About Responsibility. Be sure your grandchild knows that you are responsible for him or her, and that he or she will look to you as a parent. Make it clear that you, as a grandparent, are the one who gives permission and the one who denies it.

Have an Understanding About Money. First, you need a hard and fast understanding with your children regarding money. You can't be parents to your grandchildren unless you control the money. This is not a move to cut the parents out of their rightful place, but one that makes it possible to fill in for the parent or parents as you take on a parent role for whatever reason.

Consider Other Areas of Understanding

House space: This deals with dividing the living space and setting standards for use and cleanliness, etc.

Transportation: This deals with how all the people are going to get needed transportation, first to work, then school, then extras such as private piano lessons. Following these uses come the more pleasure-oriented ones.

Chores: Agreement about how all will share in the chores that the family knows to be necessary. Examples here are grass-cutting and handling trash and garbage.

Study time: You should establish agreements about study, giving it priority over TV or other more recreational temptations.

Recreation time: Recreation is important and should get some scheduled time every day. Recreation needs to be with other children the same age or as near as possible to the same age. You may be a stickler for a program or you might be relaxed about the type or types of exercise your grandchildren get. What is important is that they get some carefree playtime with their peers. It is O.K. for grandparents to enter into some of their recreation, yet you should be careful to let children have other children, above all else.

Regeneration time: This includes time when the family ponders its values, its worth, its direction, its contribution, its faith, and its roots. This can be a focus around Bible study or some theme of family and personal enrichment. You have a right to have an agreement for such a time.

13. Foster Grandparents

Older Americans in Action is one of the Federal Government's most productive efforts. It provides three Older American Volunteer Programs for one of America's most valuable resources—people sixty years of age and over. The programs are Retired Senior Volunteer Program (RSVP), Foster Grandparent Program (FGP), and Senior Companion Program (SCP). Two different groups of people who benefit from these services are older, low-income people who want to feel needed and lonely children institutionalized or otherwise disadvantaged who desperately need care, love, and attention.

A participant of the Foster Grandparent Program said, "I was so lonesome sitting around home, but now I look forward to being with the children every day and I enjoy being with them because they need me and I need them—we both need each other."

In a report on the Vermont Project at the Brandon Training School, Miss Carolyn Willock said:

> Everyone visiting our program is amazed at the work done by older persons and impressed by their tenacity, for twelve of

our original fifteen grandparents are still going strong in their fourth year of employment.

I'm convinced that in purely financial terms this program saves taxpayers dollars by keeping older persons independent and out of hospitals or nursing homes. Plain money given to older persons without the program involvement would not do this. (*Aging,* Feb. 1970, p. 24)

Quotes from persons who have become a part of the loving, caring, sharing life-style of Retired Senior Volunteer Program (RSVP) and Senior Companion Program (SCP) follow:

When you're growing older, there are about two ways to go. You can stay home and feel sorry for yourself or get out and see who needs you.

I think a person's first reaction to retirement is "Wow, now I can stay in bed in the mornings." That wears off pretty fast. Life needs an objective. Otherwise the gray matter just doesn't function any more.

Eighteen months ago, I was stagnated and depressed. Now things are different. I love what I'm doing. Everyone cares about everyone else, and I am active and involved and happy. (*ACTION* Pamphlet, 4500.7, June 1975; U.S. Government Printing Office, 1975)

These programs are operated in all fifty states, the District of Columbia, Puerto Rico, and the Virgin Islands. While there are no educational requirements, foster grandparents are persons over sixty years of age with low income, good health, and who have time and love to give. They receive a small stipend. Transportation is arranged. They receive a meal each day they serve and an annual physical examination.

Information about Older Americans in Action can be obtained from the following regional offices, or you may call the national office toll free (800)424-8580:

ACTION Region I, John W. McCormack Federal Bldg., Room 1420, Boston, Mass. 02109. (Connecticut, Maine, Massachusetts, New Hampshire, Rhode Island.) Phone: (617)223-4501

ACTION Region II, 26 Federal Plaza, Room 1611, New York, N.Y. 10007. (New Jersey, New York, Puerto Rico, Virgin Islands.) Phone: (212)264-5710

ACTION Region III, U.S. Custom House, Room 112, 2d and Chestnut Streets, Philadelphia, Pa. 19106. (Delaware, District of Columbia, Maryland, Pennsylvania, Virginia, West Virginia.) Phone: (215)597-9972

ACTION Region IV, 730 Peachtree Street, N.E., Room 895, Atlanta, Ga. 30308 (Alabama, Florida, Georgia, Kentucky, Mississippi, North Carolina, South Carolina, Tennessee.) Phone: (404) 526-3337

ACTION Region V, 1 North Wacker Drive, Room 322, Chicago, Ill. 60606. (Illinois, Indiana, Michigan, Minnesota, Ohio, Wisconsin.) Phone: (312)353-5107

ACTION Region VI, 212 North St. Paul Street, Room 1600, Dallas, Tex. 75201. (Arkansas, Louisiana, New Mexico, Oklahoma, Texas.) Phone: (214)749-1361

ACTION Region VII, 2 Gateway Center, 4th and State Streets, Room 330, Kansas City, Kans. 66101. (Iowa, Kansas, Missouri, Nebraska.) Phone: (816)374-4486

ACTION Region VIII, 1845 Sherman Street, Denver, Colo. 80203. (Colorado, Montana, North Dakota, South Dakota, Utah, Wyoming.) Phone: (303)327-2671

ACTION Region IX, 211 Main Street, Fifth Floor, San Francisco, Calif. 94105. (Arizona, California, Hawaii, Nevada, Guam, American Samoa.) Phone: (415)556-1736

ACTION Region X, 1601 Second Avenue, Seattle, Wash. 98101. (Alaska, Idaho, Oregon, Washington.) Phone: (206)399-4520

Community Resources

The program described is a nationwide effort to involve helping persons. At a local level, churches, community centers, and councils of churches provide opportunities for such services.

Personal Effort

Lacking such contacts, Jan Selbe wrote a delightful story in *Redbook* entitled "We Found Grandparents Through the Want-Ads." She and her husband and three children moved from Wyoming to Idaho in the late '60s. The parents divorced. Jan, in her concern for relationship for herself and children, thought of running an ad in the local paper. "Wanted—Grandmother. Mother of three wishes to make acquaintance of older woman for the purposes of family outings and emergencies." (Jan Selbe, "We Found Grandparents Through the Want-Ads," *Redbook,* Oct. 1974, pp. 42–46.)

The ad was answered by a grandmother who had two children, but they lived so many miles away she saw very little of her own grandchildren. The beautiful relationship that developed provided the children with a grandparent's home to visit, a warm, caring grandfather and grandmother to love. The story ends happily in that the parents worked out their differences and were remarried. The "newspaper grandparents" continued to be a part of their lives.

Grandparents can be working models of love and nurture in our fragmented society. Relationship does not have to depend on accident of birth, it can be born of a caring spirit.

Conclusion

The grandparenting you are doing now could be over in a few years. If it is not over, it will certainly change character. It is not the same to be a grandparent to a three-year-old as to one who is in high school or beyond.

For Mary Ben and me, the grandparenting we received in the rural South was quite different from the grandparenting we do as city dwellers in the last quarter of the twentieth century, and different from most of yours. Yet, some things change and others don't. At least the props on the stage are more sophisticated in the present generation. Perhaps we are the people who have as much interest in the nonessentials of furniture and scenery as in the movement of the play.

In our life-span Mary Ben and I have witnessed more outward changes in transportation, agriculture, medicine, engineering, and science than all the generations since the Christian era began. Yet, these changes do not change the truth about human nature. Hence our tasks as parents and grandparents may need to adjust to new realities without a

111

demand that we cut ourselves off from our roots and begin anew. We can't do that anyway.

On the positive side, modern conveniences have given grandparents respite from dawn-to-dusk labors that prevailed in the past. We are heirs of better health care and an extended life expectancy. The stage is set for us to have time with our grandchildren that was not possible two generations ago.

THINGS THAT REMAIN

Good grandparenting needs time and planning and thinking. It seldom just happens. In order to have good grandparenting it is not a must that you have affluence and opulence. What you need is alertness and care to seize upon the time available. You might need to create your own opportunities.

Childhood is childhood, and it has a remarkable sameness everywhere. Grandparents are grandparents wherever you find them. When child and grandparent get together they may have some timeless or time-filled moments. For grandparents, the child helps you "step back into the dawn," and for the child you become assurance that it's O.K. to move toward the future. No matter how young you are as a grandparent, you are a very old person to a little child. Not only are you old, you are wise—by comparison to the child. The child hungers for what you are, for what you know, and at the same time helps you recall your own dreams that just might be fulfilled in the exchanges between you.

Epilogue
To Love and Let Go

Love carries the pain of separation; the sweetness of the present is shadowed by a divided path ahead. Maybe it is tinted, even tainted, with the flow of time that annuls our unions and breaks up our clusters.

Love is a mighty witness that we exist; yet my hand is uncertain whether to grasp and hold, or to be open, yielding and freeing. Is it a vine or a tree? Will it clutch and cling or will it stand and stretch and breathe?

Love that lets go does not let itself go, but is bound by its own vows to keep a fire burning in the hearth.

Love that lets go is a patient father, a faithful mother, a committed friend. Love is present when it is needed; it is available but not in sight when it is not needed. If it is needed again, it is available. If it is needed no more, it rejoices that it was once needed.

In its youth, love is haste, speed, rush, and commotion; in its ripeness, love is patience, endurance, and kindness.

Love is the agony of freedom yearning to trespass and being restrained by its own necessity. It is the begetting power that withdraws and withholds from what it has begotten. Love is hunger to touch across the forbidden barrier and it is the restraint that often makes it unknown to its own fruit.

Because of love I know why God is unseen in a star-covered sky and unheard in the churning of the blue ocean spray. His is the love that turns loose of what he has created, leaving me to wonder, to worship, to work, to grow, to wait, and to trust.

So my love breathes and begets, and brings forth and nurtures and coddles. It sustains and soothes and supports and then silently withdraws and seems to disappear. Its eye must be no more apparent than a star behind a cloud; its arms should be as ungrappling as the branches of the oak tree; its breath may be no closer than the wind in the pine needles.

Love makes itself a stranger to what it has created; it makes itself homeless in its home; it deprives itself of its own riches; it gets no medicine in its own dispensary.

Love does not obligate; it does not manipulate; it does not dominate, conspire, cajole, or threaten.

Love is free because it is freeing. Love cannot have what it wants from the other because of what it wants for the other.

Love yearns to own and possess and control and hold, but love knows it must yield, and loose, and unbind, and let go.

So it may be with you as a grandparent; you may love, but you can't control; there is also a time when you will need to let go.

For Further Reading

BOOKS FOR JUVENILES

Adler, David A. *A Little at a Time.* Illus. by N. M. Bo-
decker. Random House, 1976.

Things grow and change a little at a time, as a grandfather
explains to grandson.

Borack, Barbara. *Grandpa.* Pictures by Ben Shecter. Harper
& Row, 1967.

Grandfather's mild and accepting manners delight a little
girl.

Cawley, Winifred. *Gran at Coalgate.* Illus. by Fermin
Rocker. Holt, Rinehart & Winston, 1975.

While recuperating from a long illness, a teenage girl goes
to live in an English coal-mining town with her grandmother.

Goldman, Susan. *Grandma Is Somebody Special.* Albert
Whitman & Co., 1976.

Hellberg, Hans Eric. *Grandpa's Maria.* Tr. from Swedish by Patricia Crampton. Illus. by Joan Sandin. William Morrow & Co., 1974.

A little Swedish girl has many adventures living with her grandfather while her mother is hospitalized.

Keller, Beverly. *Don't Throw Another One, Dover!* Drawings by Jacqueline Chevast. Coward, McCann & Geoghegan, 1976.

Upset that his mother is going to have a new baby and he must stay with his grandmother, Dover, master of the tantrum, discovers he is not the only one who can kick, growl, and howl.

Kirk, Barbara. *Grandpa, Me and Our House in the Tree.* Macmillan Publishing Co., 1978.

A small boy and his grandfather share a special relationship despite the old man's illness.

Lasky, Kathryn. *I Have Four Names for My Grandfather.* Photographs by Christopher G. Knight. Little, Brown & Co., 1976.

Monjo, Ferdinand N. *Grand Papa and Ellen Aroon: Being an Account of Some of the Happy Times Spent Together by Thomas Jefferson and His Favorite Granddaughter.* Illus. by Richard Cuffari. Holt, Rinehart & Winston, 1974.

Peck, Richard. *Monster Night at Grandma's House.* Illus. by Don Freeman. Viking Press, 1977.

Daytime at grandma's house is fine, but bedtime is terrifying when a monster seems to be about.

BOOKS FOR ADULTS

Barrett, John M. *Daniel Discovers Daniel.* Augsburg Publishing House, 1979.

Good insight into the pain of family favoritism. This book will help grandparents know the value of building self-esteem in children.

Hough, Richard, ed. *Advice to My Grand-Daughter: Letters from Queen Victoria to Princess Victoria of Hesse.* Simon & Schuster, 1976.

Hyde, Tracy Elliot. *The Single Grandmother* (How to Thrive on Your Own). Nelson-Hall Co., 1974.

Mead, Margaret. *Blackberry Winter: My Earlier Years.* Simon & Schuster, A Touchstone Book, 1972.

Olsson, Karl A. *When the Road Bends: A Book About the Pain and Joy of Passage.* Augsburg Publishing House, 1978.

Richardson, Frank Howard. *Grandparents and Their Families: A Guide for Three Generations.* David McKay Co., 1964.

Shedd, Charlie W. *Grandparents: Then God Created Grandparents and It Was Very Good.* Doubleday & Co., 1978.

Wickes, Frances G. *The Inner World of Childhood.* Appleton-Century-Crofts, 1972.